# THE FARMER'S PANTRY

THIS BOOK IS FOR OUR PARENTS,
OUR CHILDREN AND OUR FAMILIES,
AND EVERYONE WHO'S EVER MOVED,
ADAPTED AND KEPT COOKING.

FOR THE ONES WHO PASSED RECIPES
DOWN OVER DINNER TABLES,
ACROSS COUNTRIES AND THROUGH
GENERATIONS.

FOR THOSE WHO KEPT THE FLAVOURS
AND PANTRIES ALIVE.

# THE

# PANTRY

**22 STAPLE INGREDIENTS. 100 RECIPES.
MAKE GOOD FOOD, BOLD.**

Nitai Shevach, Ali Recanati + Jonathan Recanati

EBURY
PRESS

# CONTENTS

INTRODUCTION 06
EQUIPMENT 14

## Blends & Marinades 16
Baharat 18
Chermoula 26
Harissa 38
Shawarma 50
Za'atar 60
Amba 68

## Condiments & Sauces 80
Tahini 82
Miso 96
Date Molasses 104
Yeast Extract 114

## Nuts, Seeds & Crunches 122
Pitta Chips 124
Walnuts 132
Dukkah 140
Sesame Seeds 150

## Pickles & Ferments 158
Pickled Chilli & Pickled Red Onion 160
Kalamata Olives 166
Preserved Lemon 174
Gochujang 184

## Pulses, Grains & Wheat 194
Freekeh 196
Chickpeas 204
Dried Pasta 214
Flour & Bread 230

MEAL PLANS 242
INDEX 249
ACKNOWLEDGEMENTS 253

# Introduction

Our food is never boring, because we firmly believe that life's too short for bland. We want the kind of flavour that tastes like you've done loads when you've actually done very little.

We wrote this book for people who love bold food but can't be bothered with faff. People who want every meal to taste like a win, not a compromise. People who are over the beige, the boring, the 'that'll do' meals and who are ready for something better. Something vibrant – something that makes your mouth water just thinking about it.

This book isn't about perfection; it's not about how to plate your dinner for Instagram. It's about how to *want* what's on your plate. It's about giving you the tools to cook with confidence, flavour and speed. Most of all, it's about bringing a bit of Farmer J into your kitchen, without needing a twelve-hour prep list or a sous chef.

We've called it *The Farmer's Pantry* because that's where the magic happens. That's the cheat – the jars, the pastes, the spice blends and the sauces that take a Tuesday night chicken thigh and make it sing. That's what this book is built on. We've cooked every dish in here around a pantry staple, things like harissa, tahini, miso, date molasses, dukkah, gochujang. These are ingredients with character and punch – with the power to take your cooking from 'meh' to 'mate, you need to try this'.

Because here's the thing: cooking is changing. Home kitchens have got braver. We're seeing more miso in the fridge than mayo. More sesame paste than pesto. People are reaching for gochujang, za'atar, chermoula – not just because they sound trendy, but because they taste bloody good. We're not afraid of flavour any more; we're chasing it.

We wanted to create a book that reflects that, a book that says you don't need five courses or five pans. Just good ingredients, a bit of curiosity, and maybe a jar of harissa tucked in the back of the fridge.

At Farmer J, we've spent years building menus around flavour, not fuss. We take great ingredients – many of them seasonal and locally sourced from British farms – and we let them speak. We don't overwork them. We just treat them with respect and a splash of something bold. Because we actually do give a fork. About where our food comes from. About how it's cooked. And about how it makes us feel afterwards.

This cookbook is built on that same thinking, the idea that cooking should be joyful and that it should feed you properly and make you excited to sit down and eat. So, if you like the sound of chermoula fish skewers, baharat roasted lamb shanks, or tahini that gets dolloped, swirled and spiced to within an inch of its life – welcome. This is your kind of cookbook.

## THE FIELDTRAY

At Farmer J, we serve our food in something called a *Fieldtray*. A word invented by Jonathan (he made sure that was in the book, twice, actually). Just to be extra clear: Jonathan invented the word *Fieldtray*. It's basically a canteen tray, if that canteen had a thing for harissa, tahini and seasonal British produce.

A Fieldtray is built around:

- **A PROPER BASE** (grains and/or greens – something sturdy)
- **A PUNCHY MAIN** (grilled meat, fish, tofu – cooked from scratch)
- **A HOT VEG SIDE** (roasted, caramelised and dressed with intention)
- **A SAUCE** (shouldn't be optional; it's often the best bit)
- **A FRESH SALAD** (seasonal crunch)

The genius of it? It's balanced. You get the right mix of flavour, texture and colour. You feel full but not floppy. And because it's real food, cooked properly (not processed), it just happens to be pretty good for you. We don't go around preaching about health, but we do cook the kind of food your body *wants* to eat.

# The team
## From Ali

Farmer J was started in 2016 by Jonathan – my husband, the J in Farmer J and the captain of this very delicious ship. Fed up with sad sandwiches and wet lettuce masquerading as lunch, he set out to build a place that actually gave a fork. Fresh food, proper cooking, nothing beige unless it's roasted cauliflower. He's also annoyingly talented in the kitchen and happens to be an excellent CEO. Vision, spreadsheets, detail, flavour – he's got the lot.

I'm Ali, the Farmer's Wife. I joined a year later with strong opinions about pickles, a mild branding obsession, and one almost-published cookbook under my belt. I'm the CMO now, and Jonathan and I run this thing together. I'm his right-hand woman, co-pilot, chief taster and occasional disruptor (putting on raves at 10am, and that sort of thing). We make a good team.

And then there's Nitai, our genius Head of Food. Nitai trained in Lyon, opened and ran the Coal Office restaurant and now runs the flavour engine of Farmer J. He's the guy who makes you rethink everything, turning green chickpeas into a hero ingredient and putting Marmite aioli on cabbage.

Together, we wrote this book – filled with recipes from the restaurant, from our homes, and from the depths of Nitai's brain (which runs entirely on za'atar and tahini). It's practical and written for people who just want to crack on and get something delicious on the table.

These aren't random trendy ingredients, they're what we actually cook with, and what you'll find in our kitchens. So the book is organised around these hero ingredients, the things that you may have bought for one recipe but then don't know what else to do with them. You'll soon realise that these are the backbone of bold cooking – the way we get to flavour fast.

Because good food doesn't have to be complicated. And because there's no excuse for boring when the world is full of flavour.

Whether you're a pro in the kitchen or you're just beginning to get your head around cumin, *The Farmer's Pantry* has your back.

And that's Farmer J. Welcome to the table.

From left to right:
**Nitai, Ali and Jonathan**

# Why the pantry matters
## From Nitai

I remember very clearly the moment I fell in love with food. I was 15, sitting at the counter of a restaurant with my father, Eitan. It was late, and I had school the next day. But I wasn't thinking about that. I was watching.

The chef calling out orders. The bartender shaking drinks. Plates flying out, laughter rising, the printer buzzing in the background. The hum of people talking, eating, being together. It was a kind of organised chaos, and I was hooked. I remember disconnecting from the moment and just soaking in the scene. I realised then that food connects people. It brings together memories, emotions, generations. And sometimes, it's the atmosphere around the plate that stays with you longer than the dish itself.

My introduction to culinary training came in 2010, with two chef instructors, Joseph and Tamar. One of the first things they ever told me, and something that's stayed with me ever since, was this: 'To be ready to host at any moment, you need a well-stocked pantry – pulses, sauces, canned goods, and more, more, more.'

That idea stuck. The pantry, I came to understand, is the soul of a kitchen. It's where creativity begins. Where the best ideas simmer. At Farmer J, it's often where we start, with a few jars and a handful of spices. We open the cupboard and see what's possible.

This book is a reflection of that belief. A celebration of ingredients that hold stories and spark inspiration. A way to show how flavour begins long before you light the stove.

# The 'why', from the 'J'
## From Jonathan

Here are a few reasons why I started Farmer J.

First off, I've always loved food. Not just the eating, but the ingredients, the freshness, and the way a great meal can stick with you.

When I was 13, I was on a family trip in Norway. While everyone else was off exploring, I stayed back on the boat, picked up a fishing rod and caught a cod. The captain cooked it for me then and there, fresh from the sea. I was completely mesmerised. That moment blew my mind and has stayed with me ever since.

Summers growing up were spent at my grandparents' house in Long Island. They had a vegetable garden, and my grandma would send me out to pick tomatoes and basil for her caprese salad. I can still smell those tomatoes – something so simple but unforgettable.

A few years ago, I had this perfect pitta near where I grew up. I watched the woman behind the counter layer it with tahini, lamb, pickled onions, hummus, tomatoes, salt, pepper, a final flourish of tahini and a pickled chilli on top. It was like watching someone paint with flavour. And when I took that first bite, it was one of those moments where everything just felt . . . right.

Since leaving home in 2007, I've often felt something was missing, that comfort of a meal made with care, that feeling of home. Farmer J was built to bring that back. Honest food, made fresh, served with purpose. It's also about the theatre of it. I've always loved open kitchens; there's something about seeing your food being made in front of you that builds trust.

And at the heart of it all, it's the people. Watching someone enjoy a meal, that never gets old. Every new face through the door is a reminder of why we started this.

Farmer J is about real food, real people and the little moments that turn an everyday lunch into something that sticks with you.

Left:
**Classic Harissa Chicken Thighs (page 44)**

# Equipment – kit you actually need

We're not into fancy gadgets for the sake of it. This is the stuff we use every day at Farmer J, and it's the stuff you'll be glad to have in your kitchen. You don't need the full line-up from a restaurant supply catalogue, but a few well-chosen bits of kit will make you a faster, neater, happier cook. Buy once, use for ever.

**KNIVES**

Don't fall for the full block of twelve. You need three good ones and that's it. Go to a proper knife shop, not just because it's fun to talk about knives, but because you'll get good advice based on your budget. Somewhere between £30 and £60 gets you something ten times better than that blunt IKEA thing you've been using since uni.

**CHEF'S KNIFE OR SANTOKU** This is your main player. Go for something that feels good in your hand – not too big, not too flashy. Santoku can be a bit easier for beginners, but either one will do the job if it's sharp and balanced.

**PARING KNIVES** Have a couple knocking about. These act as an extension of your hand – from chopping herbs to slicing strawberries to opening Amazon boxes.

**BREAD KNIFE** It sounds boring but a proper one is a game changer. Cuts sourdough without smashing it into oblivion. Once you've had a good one, you won't go back.

**THE UNSUNG HEROES**

**MICROPLANE / FINE GRATER** You'll wonder how you lived without it. Parmesan snow, garlic paste, citrus zest – this thing's magic. Nitai's has been with him since he was a student in Lyon and is still going strong.

**TONGS** Not just for barbecue dads. Think of them as heatproof hands – essential for roasting, flipping, turning and fishing stuff out of boiling water without swearing.

**DIGITAL SCALE** Game changer. Especially if you're baking or want to cook consistently. Digital, accurate and from a proper kitchen shop – avoid the plasticky ones that eat batteries.

**MIXING BOWLS** You *can* have too many, but it's hard. Stainless steel is the way to go – easy to clean, stackable, and it doesn't hold smells. Have a few sizes. Mix in them, serve from them. You'll feel smug.

**STORAGE CONTAINERS** We've all got that Tupperware drawer of doom. Bin it. Go for stackable glass or plastic containers – same size, same lids, easy life. Your fridge will thank you.

**SMALL GLASS JAR** The most underrated tool in your kitchen. Ideal for dressings – chuck everything in, screw the lid on and shake like mad. It *properly emulsifies* – no whisk, no spills, just silky vinaigrette in seconds. Bonus points if it once held Dijon mustard.

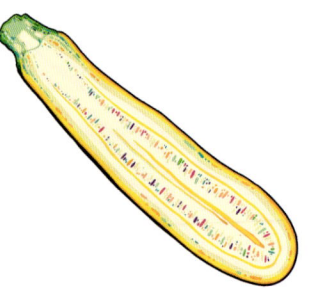

## BONUS BITS WE LOVE

**BOX GRATER** Quick, easy, does the job.

**PESTLE AND MORTAR** For smashing garlic, crushing seeds and making chimichuuri.

**GARLIC CRUSHER** If crushing with a knife isn't your thing.

**SILICONE SPATULAS** Get a few. You'll use them constantly.

**WOODEN SPOONS** Old-school but solid.

**VEG PEELER** Sharp, simple, humble.

**KITCHEN SCISSORS** Snip herbs, open bags, trim meat.

**CITRUS SQUEEZER** Gets more juice, less pips.

**FINE SIEVE** Medium size, for dressings, sauces, straining stuff.

## IF YOU'RE FEELING FANCY (OR FEEDING A CROWD)

**KITCHENAID** Not cheap, but it'll last decades. Great for cakes, doughs and, with a few attachments, you can make sausages or pasta like a pro.

**MAGIMIX** This is the king of food processors. Grates, blends, slices. Does what it says, no drama.

**HAND-HELD STICK BLENDER** Small but mighty. For soups, dressings, blitzing onions – grab one that feels solid and you'll wonder how you ever lived without it.

**THERMOMETER PROBE** Takes the guesswork out of meat. Especially handy for spatchcock chicken, no more slicing to check.

# BLENDS

# &

# *Marinades*

| Baharat | Chermoula | Harissa | Shawarma | Za'atar | Amba |
|---|---|---|---|---|---|
| *18* | *26* | *38* | *50* | *60* | *68* |

# Baharat

*adds soul to any dish*

---

Baharat is one of those spice blends that instantly wraps a dish in warmth. The name literally means 'spices' in Arabic, and every region has its own take, but the core idea is the same: deep, fragrant and slightly sweet. It's what we reach for when we want something to feel slow-cooked and comforting, even if it's not. The flavour is bold but balanced, with layers that make everything taste like it's had hours of love.

A good baharat blend usually includes black pepper, cumin, coriander, cinnamon, cloves, nutmeg, paprika, and sometimes cardamom. It's got that festive energy, like a Middle Eastern Christmas, with sweet spice sitting right alongside earthy heat. At Farmer J, our house baharat is full-bodied and unapologetically warm, with just enough punch to wake up whatever you're cooking.

We use it on everything from slow-braised lamb shanks to roast veg, stews, and even grains. It brings depth and complexity without needing to add much else. Just a spoonful turns a simple dish into something layered, rich and satisfying. It's brilliant with tomato bases, lentils, or rubbed on to chicken before roasting.

What we love most is how baharat adds soul to a dish. It's not spicy in the hot sense. It's spicy in the cosy, aromatic sense. It clings to meat, melts into sauces, and always leaves people asking what you've done to make it taste so good. The answer, most of the time? Just baharat.

# Spiced Baharat Sweet Potatoes + Yoghurt Aioli

Ve (without aioli)/ GF / DF

These are a Farmer J classic. The kind of sweet potatoes that regulars pile onto their Fieldtrays again and again – and for good reason. They're spiced, sticky, slightly crisp at the edges and soft in the middle. The baharat gives warmth, the date molasses brings a gentle sweetness; together, they do something pretty magic to a humble wedge. They're perfect with a dollop of aioli on the side.

**SERVES 4**
**PREP TIME: 15 MINS**
**COOK TIME: 25–30 MINS**

## INGREDIENTS

- 4 large sweet potatoes, skin on, scrubbed, cut into wedges
- Olive oil, enough to coat
- 2 tbsp baharat spice blend
- 2 tbsp date molasses
- Sea salt and black pepper

FOR THE YOGHURT AIOLI
- 3 egg yolks
- ½ garlic clove, crushed
- 1½ tbsp Dijon mustard
- 100ml olive oil
- 300ml neutral oil (such as avocado, pomace or sunflower oil)
- ½ tbsp red wine vinegar
- 50g Greek yoghurt

## METHOD

**1.** Preheat the oven to 200°C fan (220°C/425°F).

**2.** Cut your sweet potatoes into fat wedges – don't go too thin as you want them to hold their shape and get those nice caramelised edges. In a big bowl, toss the wedges with a good glug of olive oil, the baharat, date molasses and a generous pinch of salt and pepper. Get your hands in there and make sure everything's coated.

**3.** Line a baking tray with baking parchment (for easy clean-up) and spread the wedges out in a single layer – don't overcrowd them or they'll steam (use a second baking tray if necessary). Roast for 25–30 minutes, flipping halfway through, until golden, blistered and tender right through.

**4.** While the potatoes are roasting, make the aioli. Blitz the egg yolks, garlic and mustard in a blender. Slowly drizzle in both oils, drop by drop at first, then in a steady stream, until thick and luscious. Add the vinegar and season with a pinch of salt, then fold in the yoghurt. Taste and adjust the seasoning if needed, then store in the fridge until ready to serve.

**5.** To serve, pile up the hot potato wedges and serve with aioli on the side for dunking.

# Baharat Roasted Lamb Shanks + Mint Schug

GF / DF

This is a dish that rewards the slow, meditative process of roasting and braising to give you slow-roasted lamb shanks infused with the rich sweetness of date molasses and aromatic baharat spices, paired with minty, vibrant schug. This is elevated comfort food, perfect for cosy gatherings or a Sunday roast with flair.

**SERVES 4**
**PREP TIME: 30 MINS**
**COOK TIME: 2½ HOURS**

### INGREDIENTS
- 4 lamb shanks
- 3-4 tbsp extra virgin olive oil
- 1 white onion, roughly chopped
- 2 carrots, cut into large chunks
- 3 celery sticks, cut into large chunks
- 1 leek, trimmed and sliced into chunks
- 1 whole garlic bulb, halved horizontally
- 200ml red wine
- 2 tbsp thyme leaves
- 2 tbsp baharat spice blend
- 1 litre chicken stock (or water)
- 100g date molasses
- Sea salt and black pepper

FOR THE MINT SCHUG
- 200g flat-leaf parsley, roughly chopped
- 100g coriander, roughly chopped
- 30g mint, leaves picked
- 20g dill, roughly chopped
- 3 garlic cloves, roughly chopped
- 2 green chillies, deseeded and roughly chopped
- 1 tsp chilli flakes
- 1 whole clove
- Seeds of 3 green cardamom pods
- 2 tbsp extra virgin olive oil

### METHOD

**1.** First, make the schug. For the best flavour it needs to sit for a few hours or overnight to allow the flavours to meld – the longer it rests, the better it gets (you can also make this while the lamb shanks are in the oven). Add all the ingredients, except the olive oil, to a food processor and blend until the mixture reaches a slightly thick and chunky texture – avoid blending too long to keep that rustic, textured feel. Season to taste with salt and pepper, then transfer to a bowl and stir in the olive oil by hand, ensuring it's well combined.

**2.** Preheat the oven to 170°C fan (190°C/375°F) while you season and sear the lamb. Pat the shanks dry and season generously with salt and pepper. Heat the olive oil in a large, heavy-based cast-iron dish or casserole over a medium-high heat. Brown the shanks on all sides until golden and caramelised. This is where the flavour starts, so take your time. Once done, set them aside on a plate.

**3.** Add the onion to the same pan and cook for 2-3 minutes, allowing the onion's natural juices to deglaze the pot. Add the carrots, celery, leek and garlic and cook for an additional 5-10 minutes until slightly softened and fragrant.

**4.** Next, deglaze with wine: pour in the red wine, scraping the bottom of the pan with a wooden spoon to lift up the caramelised bits. Simmer for 2 minutes.

**5.** Return the lamb shanks to the pan, nestling them among the vegetables. Sprinkle over the thyme and baharat, then pour in the chicken stock and drizzle with date molasses. The liquid should come halfway up the shanks.

**6.** Bring everything to a simmer, cover the pan tightly with a lid and slide it into the oven. Cook for 2–2½ hours, turning the shanks halfway through, until the meat is wonderfully tender and falling off the bone.

**7.** Remove the lamb shanks and strain the cooking liquid into a separate pan. Simmer the liquid over a medium heat until reduced by half, creating a glossy, rich sauce. Taste and adjust the seasoning.

**8.** To serve, reheat the lamb shanks in the sauce, then pile them high on a large platter, drenching them in that luscious, sticky sauce. Surround them with a decent dollop of schug and enjoy.

### Tip
Texture is key for schug, so if you have a meat grinder, use it for the best consistency. You want to preserve the integrity of the herbs without turning it into a paste.

### Store
Transfer your mint schug into an airtight jar or container and refrigerate. It will keep for several days, ready to serve as a vibrant, herby condiment to accompany your dishes.

BAHARAT

# Baharat Sticky Salmon + Coriander Rice

GF / DF (if not using butter)

A sticky, spiced salmon that practically melts in your mouth, glazed in date molasses and baharat for deep, smoky sweetness. Paired with fragrant coriander rice, this is the kind of dish that looks fancy but takes no effort. Perfect for feeding a crowd.

**SERVES 5–6**
**PREP TIME: 15–20 MINS (PLUS MARINATING)**
**COOK TIME: 20 MINS**

## INGREDIENTS
- 1 whole side of salmon (1.2–1.5kg), skin on, bones removed
- 100g date molasses
- 2 tbsp soy sauce
- 1 tbsp baharat spice blend
- ½ tbsp chilli flakes
- Sea salt and black pepper

FOR THE CORIANDER RICE
- 50ml olive oil (or ghee or butter)
- 1 tbsp coriander seeds
- 400g basmati rice
- 720ml boiling water (from the kettle)
- 1 tbsp baharat spice blend
- Large bunch of fresh coriander (about 50g), finely chopped

## METHOD

**1.** Score the salmon fillet in a criss-cross pattern, cutting about halfway through the flesh but not all the way through to the skin. Season generously with salt and place it skin-side up in a large baking tray.

**2.** In a bowl, mix the date molasses, soy sauce, baharat, chilli flakes and some black pepper, then pour most of the mixture over the salmon, making sure it's evenly coated (keep back 1–2 tablespoons for drizzling once it's cooked). Cover with cling film and leave in the fridge for at least 2 hours, or overnight if you've planned ahead. You might have to carefully fold the end of the salmon on itself if it doesn't fit in your fridge! Before cooking, flip the salmon skin-side down and pour any extra marinade in the tray over the top.

**3.** When you are ready to cook, preheat the oven to 230°C fan (250°C/480°F) while you prepare the rice. Heat the olive oil (or ghee/butter) in a pan over a low heat and add the coriander seeds. Stir constantly for about 3 minutes, then add the rice and keep stirring for a minute to heat the grains.

**4.** Carefully pour the boiling water into the pan – the sizzle means you're on the right track. Increase the heat to medium and let the rice simmer before reducing it to as low as possible. Add the baharat and season with salt and pepper, stir gently, and taste the water. It should be slightly salty as the rice will absorb it while cooking. Cover with a lid and cook on low for 15–17 minutes.

**5.** Once cooked, turn off the heat and gently fluff the rice with a fork. Leave the lid half off for another 10–15 minutes to let it steam and firm up. Just before serving, stir through the chopped coriander.

**6.** While you're waiting for your rice to steam and firm, place the salmon in the oven and roast for 12–15 minutes, or until cooked through and sticky with caramelised edges. Serve the salmon straight from the tray, spooning the leftover marinade and any sticky sauce over the top. Pile the coriander rice alongside and let everyone dig in.

BAHARAT

# Baharat + Beer-braised Ox Cheeks

DF

Ox cheeks don't get enough love and that's a crying shame. They're rich and flavourful and, when slow-braised, melt into the kind of tender magic that weekends are made for. We've taken inspiration from Middle Eastern flavours here, using baharat spice for warmth, beer for boldness and a good glug of date molasses to tie it all together with a touch of sweetness. Just chuck everything in, stick it in the oven and let time do its thing. Serve whole over creamy mash or polenta or keep it rustic and toss a load of baby potatoes in with the meat from the start. Either way, you're winning.

**SERVES 4–6**
**PREP TIME: 20 MINS**
**COOK TIME: 2½–3 HOURS**

## INGREDIENTS

- 1kg ox cheeks, trimmed and cut into big chunks
- Olive oil, for searing
- 1 onion, finely chopped
- 12 garlic cloves, crushed (yes, 12 – don't skimp)
- 1 large carrot, peeled and chopped
- 1 celery stick, chopped
- 2 tbsp baharat spice blend
- 2 tbsp tomato purée
- 2 x 350ml cans of beer (preferably wheat beer)
- 50ml soy sauce
- 500ml beef stock
- 2 tbsp date molasses (or honey if you must)
- Sea salt and black pepper
- Handful of parsley, chopped, to garnish

## METHOD

**1.** Preheat the oven to 160°C fan (180°C/350°F). Pat the ox cheeks dry and season them generously with salt and pepper. Get a large, heavy-based ovenproof pan hot over a medium-high heat. Add a good glug of olive oil and brown the meat all over – you want proper colour here so do this in batches if needed. Set the meat aside once it's done.

**2.** Chuck the onion, garlic, carrot and celery into the same pan and sauté for 5–7 minutes until soft and fragrant. Stir in the baharat and tomato purée and let it all cook together for another minute or two so the spices wake up. Pour in the beer, soy sauce and beef stock, scraping up any browned bits stuck to the bottom of the pan. Stir in the date molasses and bring everything to a gentle simmer.

**3.** Return the ox cheeks to the pan and make sure they're mostly submerged in the liquid. Pop the lid on (or cover tightly with foil) and transfer to the oven. Let it braise for 2½–3 hours until the meat is meltingly tender but still holds together.

**4.** Carefully lift out the ox cheeks, then strain the cooking liquid into a saucepan and discard the solids. Simmer the sauce over a medium heat until slightly thickened; taste and adjust the seasoning. Return the meat to the sauce and let it all bubble together for 10–15 minutes. Serve scattered with parsley.

# Chermoula

*a citrus punch*

---

Chermoula is North Africa's answer to a punchy, deeply aromatic marinade, usually bright green and heavy on the herbs. But at Farmer J, we don't like to play by the rules. Instead of a fresh, perishable mix, we've taken the best elements and built them into a bold, spice-laden blend that acts as a foundation for marinades, rubs and sauces. This version leans into smoky ras el hanout, citrusy preserved lemon and rich tomato purée, giving you a shelf-stable spice mix that's ready to go whenever you need a hit of big, North African flavour.

# Chermoula Marinade

Ve / GF / DF

This chermoula is as versatile as it gets. Slather it over meat, rub over fish, or mix it with yoghurt for a killer dip. We've given you the recipe to make your own ras el hanout spice blend from scratch – it's a long list of ingredients but it will keep for a good six months in airtight jar. If you're short on time, just grab a good-quality shop-bought version and crack straight on with the marinade.

**MAKES 500ML**
**PREP TIME: 15 MINS**

## INGREDIENTS
FOR THE RAS EL HANOUT SPICE BLEND (MAKES AROUND 300G – YOU'LL ONLY NEED 75G FOR THE MARINADE)

- 10g cumin seeds
- 10g coriander seeds
- 10g fennel seeds
- 10g Aleppo shatta (or mild chilli flakes)
- 25g ground cumin
- 20g ground coriander
- 10g ground fennel
- 5g ground caraway
- 5g ground cloves
- 5g ground cinnamon
- 10g ground green cardamom
- 5g ground nutmeg
- 10g ground turmeric
- 20g sweet paprika
- 5g finely ground black pepper
- 20g dried marjoram
- 5g ground bay leaf
- 30g garlic granules
- 10g onion granules
- 30g demerara sugar
- 15g sea salt

FOR THE MARINADE
- 100g preserved lemon, finely chopped
- 75g ras el hanout (see above)
- 10g sea salt
- 2g finely ground black pepper
- 130g double-concentrated tomato purée (1 tube)
- 250ml extra virgin olive oil
- 50ml water

## METHOD

**1.** To make the ras el hanout, toast the cumin seeds, coriander seeds, fennel seeds, and Aleppo Shatta in a dry pan over a medium heat until fragrant. Let them cool slightly, then grind using a spice grinder or a mortar and pestle.

**2.** Combine all the remaining ingredients in a large bowl, including all the ground spices, dried herbs, garlic and onion granules and sugar and salt, to balance out the flavours. Add the freshly ground toasted seeds and mix everything thoroughly, then transfer to an airtight jar. Store in a cool, dry place for up to six months.

**3.** To make the marinade, put the finely chopped preserved lemons, along with any juices, into a large bowl. Mix in the ras el hanout, salt and pepper, then stir in the tomato purée until fully combined. Slowly pour in the olive oil while stirring constantly, creating a thick, glossy marinade. Gradually add the water until the mixture is smooth but still thick enough to cling to whatever you're marinating.

**4.** Taste and adjust – if you want it saltier, add more preserved lemon, if you want it richer, throw in more tomato purée. Store in an airtight container in the fridge for up to a week.

# Chermoula Fish Skewers + Blistered Greens + Lemon Zest

GF / DF

Skewered chunks of fish, bathed in punchy, fragrant chermoula and grilled until lightly charred and flaky. Paired with blistered greens, caramelised with garlic and brightened with lemon zest, this is simple, bold cooking at its best. Perfect for a summer barbecue or a quick weeknight dinner.

**SERVES 4–6**
**PREP TIME: 15 MINS (PLUS MARINATING)**
**COOK TIME: 15 MINS**

## INGREDIENTS

- 4 fish fillets (such as salmon, cod or halibut), cut into 2.5cm cubes
- 120ml Chermoula Marinade (page 27)
- 1 tbsp olive oil, for brushing
- Chopped fresh parsley, to garnish (optional)
- Lemon wedges, to serve

FOR THE BLISTERED GREENS
- 1 tbsp olive oil
- 350g green beans, trimmed
- 350g tenderstem broccoli
- 2 garlic cloves, crushed
- ¼ tsp chilli flakes (optional)
- Zest of 2 lemons, plus a squeeze of juice
- Sea salt and black pepper

## METHOD

**1.** Place the fish cubes in a bowl, pour over the chermoula marinade and toss to coat thoroughly. Cover and refrigerate for at least 30 minutes, but no longer than an hour to keep the fish tender. If you are using wooden skewers, soak them in water now to prevent them burning on or under the grill.

**2.** While the fish is marinating, start blistering the greens. Heat the olive oil in a large pan over a medium-high heat. Add the green beans and broccoli and sauté for 7–9 minutes, stirring occasionally, until they start to blister and turn golden brown. Add the garlic and chilli flakes (if using), and cook for another minute until fragrant. Season with salt and black pepper, then stir in the lemon zest. Finish with a squeeze of lemon juice and set aside.

**3.** Preheat your oven grill to high (about 220–240°C) or heat a griddle pan on the hob over a medium-high heat. Thread the marinated fish on to the skewers and brush lightly with olive oil to stop them sticking.

**4.** Cook the skewers for 3–4 minutes on each side, turning carefully, until the fish is opaque and cooked through. If you're using the oven grill, place them on a foil-lined tray and grill on the top shelf. If using a griddle pan, cook them on the hob until nicely charred and just cooked through.

**5.** Let the skewers rest for a minute, then arrange on a platter with the blistered greens. Serve with parsley, if using, and plenty of lemon wedges for squeezing over.

CHERMOULA

# Chermoula Chicken + Pickle Plate

GF / DF

Juicy, spice-packed chicken thighs grilled to perfection, drizzled with a vibrant chermoula finishing sauce and spicy green tahini. The deep, smoky flavours of the marinade are lifted by fresh lemon and finished with plenty of parsley for brightness. Served with a plate of crunchy, tangy pickles, this is bold, zesty eating at its best. The pickles develop deeper flavour the longer they sit – they need at least 24 hours to pickle properly, so plan ahead.

**SERVES 4–6**
**PREP TIME: 20 MINS (PLUS MARINATING AND PICKLING)**
**COOK TIME: 15 MINS**

## INGREDIENTS

FOR THE CHERMOULA CHICKEN THIGHS
- 8 boneless, skinless chicken thighs
- 420ml Chermoula Marinade (page 27)
- 50ml olive oil, plus extra for grilling
- 5 tbsp lemon juice
- 1g sea salt (about ¼ tsp)

FOR THE PICKLE PLATE
- ¼ head cauliflower, cut into florets
- 1 carrot, thinly sliced
- ½ stick celery, sliced
- ½ turnip, cut into small sticks
- ¼ head white cabbage, roughly chopped
- ½ red chilli, sliced
- ½ kohlrabi, cut into small sticks
- 2 garlic cloves, peeled
- 300ml water
- 30ml white wine vinegar
- 25ml lemon juice
- ½ tbsp cumin seeds
- ½ tbsp coriander seeds
- 1 green cardamom pod
- 1 sprig of dill
- 1 bay leaf
- 1 tbsp Amba Spice Blend (page 69)
- 15g sea salt
- 5g sugar

TO SERVE
- Spicy Green Tahini (page 83)
- Chopped fresh parsley
- Lemon wedges

## METHOD

**1.** Start with your pickles – you'll need to make them at least 24 hours before you want to eat them. Pack all the prepared vegetables as tightly as possible into a large glass jar – they'll shrink once the liquid is added, so don't worry if it seems full.

**2.** Combine the water, white wine vinegar, lemon juice, spices, salt and sugar in a pan and bring to the boil over a medium heat. Let it simmer for 3–5 minutes, stirring occasionally. Taste the brine, it will be strong and punchy, but it needs to be, as the vegetables will absorb the flavour as they pickle. Adjust the salt, vinegar or lemon juice if needed.

**3.** Carefully pour the hot pickle liquid over the packed vegetables, making sure they're completely submerged. You may need to press them down slightly to fit everything in. Let the jar cool to room temperature, then cover with a lid and leave at room temperature for at least 24 hours to let the flavours develop. Transfer the jar to the fridge. The pickles will be ready to eat but will continue to get better over time.

**4.** To prepare the chicken, put the chicken thighs into a bowl and pour over 120ml of the chermoula marinade, turning to make sure they're well coated. Cover and refrigerate for at least 1–2 hours, or overnight for a deeper flavour.

**5.** While the chicken is marinating, make the finishing sauce by whisking together the remaining chermoula marinade, olive oil, lemon juice and salt until smooth. Taste and adjust the seasoning as needed.

**6.** Preheat a grill to medium-high heat. If using charcoal, let the coals burn down to a glowing, ashy layer. Brush the grill grates with olive oil to prevent sticking. Remove the chicken from the marinade, letting the excess drip off, and place it on the grill. Cook for 5–6 minutes on each side until browned and cooked through.

**7.** Once cooked, let the chicken rest for a few minutes before serving. Arrange the thighs on a platter and drizzle with spicy green tahini, then scatter over the chopped parsley. Just before serving, drizzle the chermoula finishing sauce over the top, or serve it on the side for dipping. Serve with lemon wedges and a plate of pickles alongside for a sharp, crunchy contrast.

# Chermoula Lamb Chops + Mint Yoghurt

GF

Juicy, spice-infused lamb chops, grilled to perfection with smoky chermoula, balanced by a cool, creamy mint yoghurt sauce. The deep, fragrant marinade works its way into the meat, while the yoghurt sauce brings a fresh, tangy contrast. This is no-fuss, fire-kissed cooking at its finest.

**SERVES 4**
**PREP TIME: 15 MINS (PLUS MARINATING)**
**COOK TIME: 10–14 MINS**

## INGREDIENTS
- 8 lamb chops (bone-in)
- 120ml Chermoula Marinade (page 27)
- Olive oil, for brushing
- Fresh mint leaves and lemon wedges, to serve

FOR THE MINT YOGHURT SAUCE
- 240g Greek yoghurt
- 12g fresh mint, finely chopped
- 1 small garlic clove, grated
- 1 tbsp lemon juice
- 1 tbsp olive oil
- Sea salt and black pepper

## METHOD

**1.** Place the lamb chops in a bowl and pour over the chermoula marinade, making sure each chop is fully coated. Cover and refrigerate for at least 1–2 hours, or overnight if you've planned ahead.

**2.** While the lamb is marinating, make the yoghurt sauce. In a small bowl, mix the Greek yoghurt, fresh mint, garlic, lemon juice and olive oil until smooth. Season with salt and pepper, then taste and adjust if needed. Stick it in the fridge until ready to serve, to let the flavours mingle.

**3.** If using an oven, preheat it to 220°C fan (240°C/465°F). If using a grill, fire it up to a medium-high heat. If using charcoal, light the coals and let them burn down until glowing with a light layer of ash.

**4.** If grilling or barbecuing, brush the grill grates with olive oil to prevent sticking. Remove the lamb from the marinade, letting the excess drip off. Place the chops on the grill and cook for 4–5 minutes on each side for medium-rare, or 6–7 minutes on each side for medium. They should be browned and lightly charred on the outside. To roast in the oven, set a wire rack over a roasting tray, brush with oil and place the chops on top. Roast for 10–12 minutes, turning halfway through, until cooked to your liking.

**5.** Once done, let the lamb rest for 5 minutes to keep it juicy. Spread the mint yoghurt sauce on a platter and arrange the chops on top. Scatter over fresh mint leaves and serve with plenty of lemon wedges for an extra tangy hit.

CHERMOULA

# Chermoula Spatchcock Chicken + Sage Butter Potatoes

GF

This is a Sunday roast done the Farmer J way. Big flavour, no fuss, no juggling multiple pans. Spatchcocking the chicken gives you all the joy of golden, crispy skin with juicy, evenly cooked meat, and it cooks quicker, too. The chermoula brings citrus, spice and serious depth, and the sage butter potatoes? You get crispy edges, herby butter and all the flavour catching in the pan.

The marinade also works brilliantly on a classic whole roast chicken if you're not up for the spatchcock. But honestly, flattening it out gives you that extra bit of crisp and caramelisation we're always chasing. Serve it up with a spoonful of tahini on the side, because, why not? It's Farmer J. We put tahini on everything.

**SERVES 4**
**PREP TIME: 20 MINS**
**COOK TIME: 55–65 MINS**

## INGREDIENTS

- 800g baby potatoes, halved or quartered
- 1 whole chicken (1.5-2kg), spatchcocked (ask your butcher or see step 2)
- 3 tbsp Chermoula Marinade (page 27)
- 2 tbsp olive oil
- 3 tbsp unsalted butter
- 6-8 sage leaves, finely chopped (or 1 tbsp dried)
- 2 garlic cloves, crushed
- Zest of 1 lemon
- Sea salt and black pepper
- 1 lemon, cut into wedges, to serve
- Handful of chopped coriander, to garnish

## METHOD

**1.** Preheat the oven to 200°C fan (220°C/425°F). Boil the potatoes in salted water for 8-10 minutes until just tender, then drain and let them steam off.

**2.** While they're bubbling away, spatchcock your chicken if it's not already done. Put your chicken on a board, breast-side down. Use sturdy scissors to cut along each side of the backbone to remove it. Turn the chicken over, then press flat with the heel of your hand. Rub it all over with chermoula marinade, getting it right into the joints. Drizzle with olive oil, season generously, and leave it to marinate while the spuds finish.

**3.** Grab a large roasting tray. Melt the butter gently in a saucepan with the sage, garlic and lemon zest until it smells fantastic. Toss the drained potatoes in this butter, then scatter them around the tray. Nestle the chicken on top, breast-side up.

**4.** Roast for 45-55 minutes, basting halfway through with the buttery, spiced juices. You want the skin crisp and the thigh hitting 75°C (165°F) on a probe thermometer.

**5.** Let the chicken rest for 5 minutes before carving. Serve everything straight from the tray – crispy chicken, buttery sage potatoes, lemon wedges for squeezing, and coriander flung over the top.

# Esquites Corn Salad

V / GF

Think of this as Mexican street corn meets Farmer J. We stir through a good spoonful of our chermoula marinade for a citrusy, herby punch that takes this barbecue side or lunchtime salad to a whole new place. It's creamy, tangy, spicy, smoky and indulgent. Serve warm and eat it fast.

**SERVES 4**
**PREP TIME: 15 MINS**
**COOK TIME: 10–15 MINS**

## INGREDIENTS

- 4 corn cobs, husked (or use 500g frozen corn kernels)
- 1 tbsp butter
- 2 tbsp Chermoula Marinade (page 27)
- 120g sour cream
- 1 tbsp lime juice
- 1 small red chilli, thinly sliced, or ½ tsp chilli powder (or more if you're feeling brave)
- ½ tsp smoked paprika (optional)
- 30g Cotija cheese, crumbled (or use feta)
- Small handful of chopped coriander
- Sea salt and black pepper
- Lime wedges, to serve

## METHOD

**1.** If you're using corn on the cob, boil them for 7–10 minutes until just tender. If you've already got a barbecue going, get them straight on to the grill, turning now and then until the kernels are golden and charred in spots. Stand the cooked corn cobs upright on a board and use a sharp knife to slice off the kernels. If you're using frozen corn, just heat it through in a pan until warm.

**2.** Melt the butter in a frying pan over a medium heat. Add the chermoula marinade and let it sizzle for 30 seconds to wake up the spices. Tip in the cooked corn and stir to coat. Let it cook for a couple more minutes so all the flavours marry.

**3.** Meanwhile, mix the sour cream, lime juice, chilli or chilli powder and smoked paprika (if using) in a bowl and season well. Pour the creamy dressing over the warm chermoula corn and give it all a good stir.

**4.** Top with crumbled cheese, scatter over the coriander and serve with lime wedges for squeezing. Eat while warm.

CHERMOULA

# Harissa

*the heartbeat of Farmer J*

---

If there's one thing we stand by at Farmer J, it's that harissa makes everything better. This fiery, smoky, deeply spiced paste hails from North Africa, where it's been bringing heat and depth to everything from slow-cooked stews to grilled meats for centuries. Harissa is a blend of dried chillies, garlic, spices and vinegar, pounded to a thick, fragrant paste. Every region has its own version – some punchy and hot, others mild and smoky. But no matter how you make it, harissa is all about bold, unapologetic flavour. We love it because it's the workhorse of the kitchen. Smear it on to chicken before roasting, stir it through soups for a deep, smoky warmth, or mix it with yoghurt for a quick, creamy marinade that transforms anything it touches. It's the backbone of our Harissa Chicken, the dish that put Farmer J on the map: charred, juicy and packing just the right amount of heat. And the best part? Once you've got a jar in the fridge, you're never more than a spoonful away from turning the most basic meal into something knockout. Stir it into beans, melt it into a cheese toastie, or dollop it into a bubbling shakshuka. This stuff brings instant attitude to anything.

# Farmer J's Harissa

Ve / GF / DF

From the day we opened Farmer J, we made harissa from scratch, blending chillies we sourced from all over the world. No shortcuts, no shop-bought pastes; just proper, fiery harissa the way it should be. For as long as Farmer J has existed, we have always joked that if you spend too long here, you don't just eat harissa, you become harissa. The smell clings to your clothes, your hair, and possibly your soul. We wear it like a badge of honour. Make this recipe, and before long, you'll be walking around smelling like smoky, spicy greatness too.

**MAKES 1 JAR (250ML)**
**PREP TIME: 5 MINS (PLUS SOAKING)**

## INGREDIENTS

- 100g dried sweet or hot peppers
- 4 garlic cloves, crushed
- ¼ tsp ground cumin
- ¼ tsp ground caraway (or coriander)
- ½ tsp sea salt
- 1 tsp white wine vinegar
- 60ml neutral oil (such as avocado, pomace or sunflower oil), plus extra for sealing the jar
- 1 tbsp coriander seeds lightly toasted and crushed (optional)

## METHOD

**1.** Cut off the stems of the dried peppers using scissors or a knife, then split them open and remove the seeds. If you're using hot peppers, wear gloves to avoid burning your eyes. Wash the peppers under running water, then place them in a large bowl and cover with cold water. Weigh them down with a plate to keep them submerged and let them soak for 1 hour.

**2.** Drain the peppers and lay them on a towel lined with kitchen paper, then pat them dry. Chuck them into a food processor along with the garlic, cumin, caraway, salt and vinegar. Blitz until a rough paste starts to form, scraping down the sides as needed. With the processor running, slowly drizzle in the oil and keep blending until you get a smooth, thick paste. Stir in the crushed coriander seeds (if using) for extra depth.

**3.** Spoon the harissa into a clean jar and pour a thin layer of oil over the top to keep it fresh. Store in the fridge and use it on everything: grilled meat, eggs, roasted veg, beans, toasties, shakshuka, or straight off the spoon if you're that way inclined. This stuff only gets better with time. It'll keep in the fridge for up to 3–4 weeks – just make sure you use a clean spoon each time and top it up with a fresh layer of oil if needed.

# Harissa Baked Beans, Labneh, Preserved Lemon + Poached Egg

V

This is what happens when baked beans grow up. Smoky, spiced harissa beans piled on to crisp sourdough, mellowed out with creamy labneh and brightened with sharp preserved lemons. A soft poached egg on top? That's just showing off. Perfect for breakfast, brunch, or even a lazy, no-fuss dinner, when all you want is something hearty with a bit of gumption.

**SERVES 2–3**
**PREP TIME: 10 MINS**
**COOK TIME: 20 MINS**

### INGREDIENTS
FOR THE BAKED BEANS
- 1 tbsp olive oil
- 1 small onion, finely chopped
- 2 garlic cloves, crushed
- 1 tsp ground cumin
- 1 tsp smoked paprika
- 1 tbsp tomato purée
- 75g Smoky Honey Harissa (page 43)
- 120ml vegetable stock (or water)
- 400g tin white beans (cannellini or navy), drained and rinsed
- Sea salt and black pepper

FOR THE SOURDOUGH AND TOPPINGS
- Splash of vinegar (optional)
- 2-3 eggs
- 2 slices of sourdough bread
- 3 tbsp labneh (see below)
- 2-3 preserved lemons, thinly sliced
- Chopped chives
- Olive oil, for drizzling
- Fresh parsley (optional)

### METHOD

**1.** Heat the olive oil in a saucepan over a medium heat. Add the chopped onion and sauté for 5-7 minutes until soft and caramelised. Stir in the garlic, cumin and smoked paprika and cook for another minute until fragrant. Add the tomato purée and smoky honey harissa, then pour in the vegetable stock and cook for 2-3 minutes.

**2.** Tip in the drained white beans, stir well, and let them simmer for 10-15 minutes until the sauce thickens and coats the beans. Season to taste with salt and black pepper.

**3.** Meanwhile, bring a pan of water to a gentle simmer and add a splash of vinegar if you like: it helps the eggs hold their shape. Crack each egg into a small bowl, then carefully slide them into the water. Poach for 3-4 minutes for whites that are just set and still-soft yolks. Lift out with a slotted spoon and drain on kitchen paper.

**4.** Toast the sourdough until golden and crisp. Spread each slice with a thick layer of labneh, then spoon over the harissa beans. Carefully place a poached egg on top, scatter over the preserved lemons and chopped chives, and drizzle with olive oil. If you're feeling fancy, finish with a sprinkle of fresh parsley.

**5.** Eat straight away, ideally with a knife, a fork, and a smug grin.

HOW TO MAKE
**LABNEH**

Labneh is salted Greek yoghurt left to strain until thick, creamy and spreadable. Mix ½ tsp salt into 500g full-fat Greek yoghurt, spoon into muslin or a clean tea towel, tie it up and hang over a bowl in the fridge. Leave 12-24 hours. Once thick, transfer to a container, drizzle with olive oil and keep chilled. Smear on toast, veg or meat.

HARISSA

# Harissa Fennel Salad

V / GF / DF

This salad is so much more than a side. It's punchy, sweet and bright and pairs perfectly with a toastie (you'll find our version on page 117). The fennel stays crisp, the orange adds a juicy hit of brightness, and the harissa vinaigrette brings the whole thing to life.

**SERVES 2–3**
**PREP TIME: 10 MINS**

## INGREDIENTS
- 1 orange
- 1 fennel bulb, trimmed and thinly sliced
- 6-8 black olives, pitted and chopped
- 2 spring onions, thinly sliced
- Small handful of fresh dill, chopped

FOR THE HARISSA VINAIGRETTE
- 2 tbsp Smoky Honey Harissa (page 43)
- 1 garlic clove, crushed
- 2 confit garlic cloves (or use roasted garlic)
- 1 tbsp Dijon or wholegrain mustard
- 1 tbsp lemon juice
- 1 tbsp pomegranate molasses
- 1 tbsp white wine vinegar
- 200g neutral oil (such as avocado, pomace or sunflower oil)
- Sea salt and black pepper

## METHOD

**1.** For the vinaigrette, put the harissa, garlic (both raw and confit), mustard, lemon juice, pomegranate molasses and vinegar into a small bowl and whisk until smooth. Slowly stream in the oil, whisking constantly to emulsify. Season with salt and pepper.

**2.** Segment your orange by peeling it, removing the pith and cutting out the segments with a sharp knife.

**3.** In a big bowl, toss the fennel, chopped olives, orange segments, spring onions and dill until evenly combined. Pour over the vinaigrette and toss again until everything's glistening and coated.

# Smoky Honey Harissa

V / GF / DF

If you're looking to up your harissa game, let us introduce this pimped-up version that balances deep, smoky heat with a hit of sweetness. It's got layers of flavour from dried Mexican chillies, warm spices and a drizzle of honey that rounds everything out.

**MAKES 1–2 JARS (APPROX. 450ML TOTAL)**
**PREP TIME: 10 MINS (PLUS SOAKING)**

## INGREDIENTS

- 175g dried Mexican chillies, soaked (we use a mix: 140g guajillo, 15g árbol, 20g ancho)
- 1 tsp coriander seeds
- 1½ tsp cumin seeds
- 1 tsp black pepper
- ½ tsp ground cinnamon
- 1 tsp onion granules
- 1¼ tsp ground allspice
- 190g Farmer J's Harissa (page 39)
- 1 tsp sea salt
- ¼ tsp smoked paprika
- 1 tbsp honey
- 3 tbsp neutral oil (such as avocado, pomace or sunflower oil), plus extra for topping

## METHOD

**1.** Soak the dried chillies in warm water for 30 minutes, then drain. Meanwhile, grind the coriander seeds, cumin seeds, black pepper, cinnamon and onion granules to a fine powder using a spice grinder or a mortar and pestle.

**2.** Add the soaked and drained chillies to a blender or food processor with all the remaining ingredients including the Farmer J's Harissa, except the oil, and blend until a thick paste forms. Slowly drizzle in the oil while blending, scraping down the sides as needed, until smooth and spreadable.

**3.** Transfer to a clean jar and store in the fridge for up to 2–3 weeks. To keep it fresh for longer, cover the top with a thin layer of oil.

# Classic Harissa Chicken Thighs

GF / DF

This is the dish that built Farmer J. Spicy, smoky, ridiculously juicy chicken thighs marinated in our signature harissa – cooked hot and fast until charred at the edges, tender in the middle, and ready to be drenched in more harissa and dolloped with creamy tahini. It's everything we love in a dish: bold flavour, zero fuss and something you can eat any day of the week. We've sold more of this than anything else, and once you make it at home, you'll see why. Serve it with your choice of grains and vegetables, as we've done here.

**SERVES 3–4**
**PREP TIME: 5 MINS (PLUS MARINATING)**
**COOK TIME: 25–30 MINS**

## INGREDIENTS
- 500g boneless, skinless chicken thighs
- 100g Smoky Honey Harissa (page 43), plus extra for drizzling
- 1–2 tsp neutral oil (for pan cooking)

TO SERVE
- Chopped fresh parsley
- Spicy Green or Classic Tahini (page 83)

## METHOD

**1.** Rub the chicken thighs all over with the harissa paste – you want them properly coated so don't be shy, get in there. Cover and pop in the fridge for at least an hour, but overnight is even better if you've got the time.

**2.** When you're ready to cook, choose your method: for oven roasting, preheat the oven to 200°C fan (220°C/425°F) and roast the chicken on a lined tray for 25–30 minutes, flipping halfway through. For extra char, whack it under a hot grill for the last couple of minutes. If you're using a griddle pan, place it over a medium-high heat, drizzle in a little oil, and cook the thighs for about 6–7 minutes on each side, or until they're browned and cooked through (the internal temperature should hit 75°C (165°F) on a probe thermometer.

**3.** Once cooked, rest the chicken for a couple of minutes, then pile on to a plate, scatter with chopped parsley, and drizzle with tahini and more harissa. Serve with your choice of grains and vegetables and tuck in while it's still sizzling. A total knockout.

HARISSA

# Whole Roasted Harissa Cauliflower + Spicy Green Tahini

Ve / GF / DF

This dish turns cauliflower into a total showstopper. It's bold, it's beautiful, and it's the kind of thing that looks like you've put in loads of effort, but really, it's all about a brilliant marinade and letting the oven do the work. The harissa sesame dressing clings to every crevice of the cauliflower, roasting into a caramelised, nutty crust. And that spicy green tahini? Creamy, punchy and bright as anything. Spoon it on generously. It's hearty, vibrant, and – honestly – tastes even better than it looks.

**SERVES 4–6**
**PREP TIME: 15 MINS (PLUS MARINATING)**
**COOK TIME: 30 MINS**

## INGREDIENTS

- 2 whole cauliflowers, washed, with a few green leaves left on
- 15g coriander seeds
- 5g cumin seeds
- 10g sea salt
- 100–150g Farmer J's Harissa (page 39)
- Pinch of ground cumin
- 100ml extra virgin olive oil
- 50g sesame seeds (mix of white and black)

### TO SERVE
- Chopped fresh parsley
- Thinly sliced spring onions
- Spicy Green Tahini (page 83)

## METHOD

**1.** Bring a big pan of salted water to the boil – it needs to be big enough to hold both whole cauliflowers. Lower in the cauliflowers and cook for 7–8 minutes, just until a knife slides in with a bit of resistance. You want them tender but not falling apart. Carefully lift them out and let them steam dry in a colander for 10–15 minutes, then pat them down with a clean tea towel to make sure there's no moisture hanging about. This is key as wet cauliflower won't roast properly.

**2.** While the cauliflower's drying off, crush the coriander seeds, cumin seeds and sea salt in a mortar and pestle (or spice grinder if you prefer). Stir in the harissa, ground cumin and olive oil and whisk or blend until smooth. Mix in the sesame seeds.

**3.** Place the dried cauliflowers in a large lined roasting tray or dish and brush generously with half the dressing, making sure to coat every surface and sneak some between the leaves. Let them marinate for at least 30 minutes to soak up the flavour.

**4.** Preheat the oven to 180°C fan (200°C/400°F). Roast the cauliflowers for 30 minutes, basting once or twice with some of the reserved dressing, until golden, crisp and caramelised in spots.

**5.** Remove from the oven, drizzle with more of the dressing, and scatter over fresh parsley and sliced spring onions. Serve whole at the table or cut into wedges – just be ready for it to disappear fast. And don't forget to serve it with a big bowl of spicy green tahini on the side. It's the perfect creamy, fiery contrast and takes the whole thing over the top.

# Harissa Shakshuka + Fresh Market Salad

V / GF (without bread)

This is our kind of brunch. Or lunch. Or dinner, really. Slow-cooked red peppers and onions; smoky harissa; sweet tomatoes; and eggs with golden yolks that beg for a good hunk of bread. We finish it with a scatter of crumbled feta, a swoosh of tahini on the side, and a sharp, herby market salad to cut through the richness. It's comfort food you can eat by the panful.

**SERVES 4–6**
**PREP TIME: 20 MINS**
**COOK TIME: 45–60 MINS**

### INGREDIENTS

- 2 tbsp olive oil
- 2 red onions, thinly sliced
- 4 red peppers, deseeded and thinly sliced
- 3 garlic cloves, crushed
- 1 tsp ground cumin
- 1 tsp smoked paprika
- 2 tbsp tomato purée
- 100g Smoky Honey Harissa (page 43)
- 2 x 400g tins chopped tomatoes
- 6 free-range eggs
- 100g feta cheese, crumbled
- Large handful of chopped parsley and coriander
- 3 tbsp Classic Tahini (page 83)
- Sea salt and black pepper
- Crusty sourdough or flatbreads, to serve

FOR THE MARKET SALAD

- 1 small cucumber, roughly chopped
- 200g cherry tomatoes, halved
- 1 red onion, finely chopped
- 1 red chilli, thinly sliced (optional)
- ½ lemon, thinly sliced
- 1 small fennel bulb, thinly sliced
- Handful of radishes, quartered
- Handful of Kalamata olives
- Small bunch of fresh mint, leaves picked
- Small bunch of flat-leaf parsley, roughly chopped
- Juice of 1–2 lemons
- 2 tbsp olive oil

### METHOD

**1.** Heat the olive oil in a large frying pan or shallow casserole over a medium heat. Add the onions and red peppers with a pinch of salt and cook them low and slow, for 20–25 minutes, until completely soft and sweet. Stir in the garlic, cumin and smoked paprika, letting them toast for a minute before adding the tomato purée and harissa. Let everything darken slightly, then pour in the chopped tomatoes. Simmer for 15–20 minutes until the sauce is thick and deep in flavour.

**2.** Use a spoon to make six little wells and crack an egg into each one. Cover and cook gently for 6–8 minutes, or until the whites are just set but the yolks are still soft.

**3.** While the eggs cook, make the salad: toss together the cucumber, tomatoes, red onion, chilli (if using), lemon slices, fennel, radishes, olives, mint and parsley in a bowl. Dress with the juice of one of the lemons, the olive oil and some salt and pepper. Let it sit for 5 minutes so the flavours get to know each other, then taste and adjust the seasoning, adding more lemon if needed..

**4.** Take the shakshuka off the heat and top with crumbled feta and chopped herbs. Spoon the tahini over the shak. Serve hot, with crusty sourdough or flatbread for mopping up every last bit, and that crisp, herby salad on the side for balance. This one's a crowd-pleaser, no question.

HARISSA

# Shawarma

*big flavour, no apologies*

---

Shawarma spice is straight-up flavour. There's nothing shy or subtle about it; it hits you with warmth, smoke, a little sweetness, and a depth that makes everything taste like it's been cooked over hot coals, even if it hasn't. Traditionally used to season the meat stacked and roasted on a spit, we've found it's just as good rubbed on to veg or used as a dry marinade.

A classic shawarma blend usually includes cumin, coriander, paprika, turmeric, cinnamon, garlic, and sometimes a touch of allspice or clove. It's bold, complex and full of attitude. At Farmer J, we love it most for its versatility: it brings instant energy to roasted roots, mushrooms, aubergine, or even just stirred into a pot of rice. It's the shortcut to that proper street-food depth of flavour.

What we've come to realise is that anything with shawarma spice just happens to pair perfectly with tahini. It's like they were made for each other. So whether it's chicken, veg, or skewered mushrooms, we're always reaching for the tahini to finish things off.

# Shawarma Roasted Roots, Feta + Dukkah

V / GF

Sweet, caramelised root veg roasted in warm shawarma spices, crumbled feta melting over the top, and a generous handful of homemade dukkah for crunch. Add a hit of lemon and a pop of parsley, and you've got a tray of pure roasted glory. It's earthy, nutty, spiced and bright all in one, great as a main, perfect on the side, and just as good cold the next day (if there's any left).

**SERVES 4–6**
**PREP TIME: 20 MINS**
**COOK TIME: 40 MINS**

## INGREDIENTS

- 3 large carrots, peeled and cut into thick wedges
- 3 large parsnips, peeled and cut into thick wedges
- 2 medium beetroots, peeled and cut into wedges
- 1 large sweet potato, cut into thick rounds
- 3 tbsp olive oil
- 2 tbsp Shawarma Marinade (page 56) or shop-bought shawarma spice blend
- 100g feta cheese, crumbled
- Handful of fresh parsley, chopped
- 2 tbsp Dukkah (page 141)
- Zest and juice of 1 lemon
- Sea salt and black pepper

## METHOD

**1.** Preheat the oven to 200°C fan (220°C/425°F). Add the carrots, parsnips, beets and sweet potato to a large bowl with the olive oil, shawarma marinade, salt and black pepper and toss until evenly coated. Spread out on a lined baking tray and roast for 30–40 minutes, flipping halfway through, until golden, caramelised and tender right through.

**2.** Once the roots are out of the oven, arrange them on a big platter. Scatter over the crumbled feta, chopped parsley and a generous spoonful of dukkah. Finish by grating over the lemon zest and adding a good squeeze of juice. Serve warm, with spoons at the ready.

# Aubergine Shawarma Pitta

V / DF

This is our twist on a Levantine street food icon. Instead of deep-frying aubergine, we toss it in warm, smoky shawarma spices and roast it until golden and soft. Then we pile it into fluffy, warm pittas with creamy tahini, sharp pickles, sumac onions, boiled egg and potato slices, layering everything with care to get that ideal bite: rich, herby, tangy, soft and crunchy all at once. Serve it up as a brunch or make mini versions for a sharing-style feast with friends. Either way, it'll get messy, and that's the point.

**SERVES 4–6**
**PREP TIME: 25 MINS (PLUS PICKLING)**
**COOK TIME: 30 MINS**

## INGREDIENTS

- 3 large aubergines
- 2–3 tbsp Shawarma Marinade (page 56) or shop-bought shawarma spice blend
- Olive oil, for drizzling
- 1 red onion, thinly sliced
- 1 tsp sumac
- Juice of 1 lemon
- 4–6 good-quality pittas
- 3 tbsp Classic or Spicy Green Tahini (page 83)
- 2 hard-boiled eggs, sliced and dusted with ground cumin
- 1–2 cooked potatoes (boiled or roasted), sliced
- 2 baby cucumbers, thinly sliced
- 2 ripe tomatoes, sliced
- A few fresh mint leaves (2–3 per pitta)
- Small bunch of flat-leaf parsley, chopped
- 2 tbsp Mint Schug (page 20)
- Sea salt and black pepper

## METHOD

**1.** Preheat the oven to 200°C fan (220°C/425°F). Peel alternate strips off the aubergines so they end up striped, then cut into thick slices. Toss the aubergine slices in a large bowl with the shawarma marinade, drizzle with olive oil and season with salt and pepper. Spread out on a lined baking tray and roast for 25–30 minutes, flipping once, until golden and soft but with a bit of char. Let them cool slightly on a wire rack so they don't steam and go soggy.

**2.** Meanwhile, add the sliced red onion to a bowl with the sumac, lemon juice and ½ teaspoon of sea salt. Massage gently with your hands until the onion softens, then let it sit for 30 minutes to pickle.

**3.** Warm your pittas; use a steamer if you've got one, or wrap them in a clean tea towel and microwave according to the packet instructions.

**4.** To build the pitta, start with a spoonful of tahini sauce. Add a few slices of roasted aubergine, then layer in the egg, potato, cucumber, tomato, mint and parsley. Add a spoonful of pickled sumac onions, finish with a drizzle of schug and another hit of tahini if you're feeling bold.

**5.** Serve warm, napkin in hand. Messy is part of the charm.

SHAWARMA

# Shawarma Shroom Skewers + Spicy Green Tahini

Ve / GF (without bread) / DF

These meaty, smoky, spiced mushrooms straight off the grill are definitely a crowd-pleaser. We're taking our classic shawarma-style mushrooms and threading them on to skewers for extra char and ease of serving. The mix of oyster, king oyster, shiitake and portobello gives loads of texture and depth, but use whatever mushrooms you've got kicking about. Finished with fresh parsley and a squeeze of lemon, these absolutely must be served with a big, green spoonful of our spicy tahini sauce on the side. Perfect on their own, stuffed into pittas, or alongside a big pile of grains or greens.

**SERVES 4–6 AS A SIDE OR PART OF A SPREAD**
**PREP TIME: 10 MINS**
**COOK TIME: 15–20 MINS**

## INGREDIENTS

- 500g mixed mushrooms (oyster, king oyster, shiitake, portobello or whatever you've got)
- 3 tbsp olive oil
- 1½ tbsp Shawarma Marinade (page 56) or shop-bought shawarma spice blend
- 1 tbsp chopped fresh parsley
- Sea salt

TO SERVE
- Lemon wedges
- Spicy Green Tahini (page 83)
- Pitta or flatbread

## METHOD

**1.** If you are using wooden skewers, soak them in water first to prevent them burning on or under the grill.

**2.** Tear any mushrooms on the larger side into chunky, skewer-friendly pieces. In a large bowl, toss them with the olive oil, shawarma marinade and a generous pinch of sea salt until they're well coated. Thread them on to 4–6 skewers, packing them in but not too tightly – you want to give them a bit of space so they roast, not steam.

**3.** Preheat a grill to medium-high heat. If using charcoal, let the coals burn down to a glowing, ashy layer. Cook the skewers for 15–20 minutes, turning occasionally, until the mushrooms are golden, tender and slightly charred at the edges. (Alternatively, roast the skewers on a parchment-lined tray in an oven preheated to 200°C fan (220°C/425°F) for 18–20 minutes, turning once halfway through. You're aiming for golden, tender mushrooms with slightly crisp edges, a similar finish to grilling, but a little less smoky.)

**4.** Pile on to a platter, scatter with chopped parsley and serve with lemon wedges for squeezing. Don't forget the spicy green tahini on the side – it's creamy, fiery and makes the mushrooms sing.

# Slow-cooked Lamb Shoulder + All the Toppings

This is the shawarma of dreams. Slow-cooked lamb shoulder, falling apart and full of shawarma spice, stuffed into warm pitta with every topping under the sun. We've got creamy tzatziki, crunchy cabbage salad, fiery schug, sticky-spicy tomatoes, punchy sumac onion, cooling cucumber, tangy amba, and a heavy hand of fresh herbs. Every bite is rich, cool, hot, sharp and comforting.

Yes – the ingredient list is long. It's a crazy amount of components, but you're making a proper feast here – perfect for a special occasion, a weekend celebration, or a gathering where everyone gets stuck in and builds their own. Crack open the arak and let people pile up their pittas however they like. This is how we do a celebration at Farmer J. (Image overleaf)

**SERVES 6–8**
**PREP TIME: 30 MINS (PLUS MARINATING)**
**COOK TIME: 4½–5 HOURS**

## INGREDIENTS
- 1.5–2kg lamb shoulder (bone-in)
- 4 garlic cloves, grated
- 2 tbsp ground cumin
- 1 tbsp ground coriander
- 1 tbsp paprika
- 1 tsp ground turmeric
- 1 tsp ground cinnamon
- 1 tsp ground allspice
- 1 tbsp dried oregano
- 2 tsp salt
- 1 tsp black pepper
- 60ml olive oil
- Juice of 1 lemon
- 60g natural yoghurt (optional, for extra tenderness)
- 1 tbsp honey (optional, for sweetness)

FOR THE SHAWARMA MARINADE
- 60ml olive oil
- 3 tbsp lemon juice
- 1 tbsp apple cider vinegar
- 2 tbsp ground cumin
- 2 tbsp paprika
- 1 tsp ground cinnamon
- 1 tsp ground turmeric
- 2 garlic cloves, grated
- 1 tsp salt
- ½ tsp black pepper

FOR THE PARMESAN POTATOES
- 1kg baby potatoes
- Sea salt, for boiling
- 50g butter, plus extra for dotting on top
- 80g Parmesan, finely grated

FOR THE SUMAC ONIONS
- 1 large onion, thinly sliced
- 1 tbsp sumac
- Juice of 1 lemon
- 1 tbsp olive oil
- A good pinch of sea salt

FOR THE FRESH CABBAGE SALAD
- 1 small cabbage, finely shredded
- 4 tbsp lemon juice
- 1 tbsp olive oil
- Handful of fresh parsley, roughly chopped

FOR THE SPICY TOMATOES
- 1 tbsp olive oil
- 5 medium tomatoes, quartered
- 1 red chilli, finely sliced
- 10g fresh coriander, roughly chopped

TO SERVE
- Pittas or flatbreads
- Hummus (page 205)
- Tzatziki (page 74)
- Amba sauce (shop-bought)
- Mint Schug (page 20)
- Sliced cucumber
- Pickles

**METHOD**

**1.** Rub the lamb shoulder with the garlic, ground spices, dried oregano, salt, pepper, olive oil, lemon juice, yoghurt and honey (if using). Leave to marinate for at least 2 hours, overnight if you can.

**2.** Preheat the oven to 160°C fan (180°C/350°F). Place the lamb in a roasting tray, mix together all the shawarma marinade ingredients and pour over the top of the lamb. Cover tightly with foil and roast for 4½–5 hours, basting occasionally, until the lamb is fall-apart tender. Let it rest for 20 minutes, then shred with two forks, spooning over some of the juices.

**3.** While the lamb is roasting, get going on your potatoes. Preheat your oven to 220°C fan (240°C/465°F) and boil your baby potatoes in salted water for 15–20 minutes until tender. Drain, then toss into a buttered baking dish, mix in the rest of the butter, and lightly smash each potato with the base of a mug. Grate the Parmesan over the top and roast for 20–25 minutes until golden, crispy and irresistible.

**4.** Make your toppings. Toss the sliced onion with the sumac, lemon juice, olive oil and salt and let it sit and soften. Toss the cabbage with the lemon juice, olive oil and parsley and season with salt and pepper. For the spicy tomatoes, mix the olive oil, tomatoes, chilli and coriander in a small bowl.

**5.** Warm your pittas or flatbreads and get ready to assemble. Spread a warm pitta with hummus. Add a good mound of the shredded lamb. Load up with sumac onion, a big spoonful of tzatziki, cabbage salad, spicy tomatoes, a drizzle of amba and a spoonful of mint schug. Garnish with cucumber slices and pickles.

SHAWARMA

# Za'atar

*earthy, bright and addictive*

---

Za'atar isn't just a spice, it's a way of life across the Levant. You'll find it sprinkled over breakfast, baked into breads, stirred into oil for dipping, or scattered over roast meats and veg. And it's not one single *thing*: it's a herb, a spice blend and a flavour all of its own. At its heart is a wild herb also called za'atar, part of the oregano and thyme family, with a bright, earthy and slightly lemony flavour. Some people confuse it with thyme or oregano, but proper za'atar leaves have their own unique edge – fragrant, savoury and a little wild.

The za'atar spice blend we all know and love is made by combining those dried za'atar leaves with toasted sesame seeds, sumac and a bit of salt. Some versions add marjoram or thyme, and everyone swears theirs is the best. At Farmer J, we keep ours punchy and well balanced. Nutty from the sesame, tangy from the sumac, and lifted by the herb itself. It's the kind of thing you'll start adding to everything once it's in your cupboard.

We love za'atar because it enhances without overpowering. Sprinkle it over eggs, mix it into salads, rub it on to flatbreads before baking, or stir it into olive oil for a quick dip. It's brilliant on roast veg, grilled chicken, or yoghurt. What it does is bring depth and brightness in equal measure, giving simple dishes a layer of complexity that tastes like you've done more than you have. Once you've got the flavour locked into your cooking, you'll start reaching for it instinctively. Just don't ask us to choose between za'atar and harissa – we're not ready for that kind of decision.

# Green Za'atar Shakshuka

GF (without bread)

Comforting but fresh, creamy but still packing a proper punch. Instead of the usual tomato base, we slow things down with soft greens, fresh za'atar (or oregano if you can't find it) and warm cumin, all cooked into a rich, herby sauce. Crack in some eggs, top with feta and Parmesan, and let it all bubble together until it's begging for a bit of bread to mop it up. It's a brunch showstopper, but honestly, I quite like it for dinner: warm, filling and easy to throw together at the end of the day.
(Image on page 157)

**SERVES 4**
**PREP TIME: 15 MINS**
**COOK TIME: 20–25 MINS**

### INGREDIENTS
- 2 tbsp olive oil
- 1 large shallot, finely chopped
- 3 garlic cloves, crushed
- Handful of fresh oregano leaves, chopped (if you can find fresh za'atar, leaves even better!)
- Bunch of Swiss chard (green part only), chopped
- 2 big handfuls of spinach
- ½ tsp cumin seeds
- 100ml vegetable stock
- 100ml double cream
- 8 free-range eggs
- 50g feta cheese, crumbled
- 30g Parmesan, grated
- A few fresh basil leaves
- 1 tbsp za'atar spice blend
- Sea salt and black pepper
- Warm pittas or sourdough, to serve

### METHOD

**1.** Heat the olive oil in a large cast-iron or ovenproof frying pan over a medium heat. Add the chopped shallot and garlic and sauté for 2–3 minutes until soft and fragrant. Stir in the chopped oregano, Swiss chard and spinach. Let it all cook down for a few minutes until completely wilted. Add the cumin seeds and toast for 30 seconds, just until aromatic.

**2.** Pour in the veg stock and cream, give it a stir and let it simmer for 5 minutes until thickened slightly. Season with salt and pepper.

**3.** Use a spoon to make eight little wells in the sauce and gently crack in the eggs. Use the tip of a knife to swirl the egg whites slightly into the sauce, but don't touch the yolks. Cover the pan and cook over a low heat for 5 minutes until the whites are nearly set but the yolks are still soft. Meanwhile, preheat the oven to 200°C fan (220°C/425°F).

**4.** Sprinkle over the feta, Parmesan and a few torn basil leaves, then slide the pan into the hot oven for 3–4 minutes, just to finish setting the eggs and melt the cheese.

**5.** Take it straight to the table, dust generously with za'atar and serve hot, with warm bread on the side. A spoonful of schug or a drizzle of olive oil over the top wouldn't hurt either.

# Yellow Courgette, Green Bean + Za'atar Salad

Ve / GF / DF

This is the kind of salad that eats like a proper meal. There's texture from crunchy cabbage and chickpeas, brightness from lemon and herbs, and the kick of pickled onion and pickled chilli just waking everything up. Roasted za'atar chickpeas give it body, while the yellow courgette and green beans keep things fresh and light. We love this as a main piled high in a bowl, or as a side to balance out something rich and roasted. It's herby, punchy and full of flavour.

**SERVES 4–6**
**PREP TIME: 25 MINS (PLUS PICKLING)**
**COOK TIME: 10 MINS**

## INGREDIENTS

FOR THE ZA'ATAR CHICKPEAS
- 400g tin cooked chickpeas, drained and rinsed
- 1 tbsp za'atar spice blend
- 1½ tbsp olive oil
- Sea salt

FOR THE PICKLED RED ONION
- 240ml white wine vinegar
- 240ml water
- 50g sugar
- 15g salt
- 1 large red onion, thinly sliced

FOR THE LEMON & OREGANO DRESSING
- 180ml olive oil
- 60ml lemon juice
- 1 tsp Dijon mustard
- 1½ tsp salt
- 1 garlic clove, grated
- 1 tbsp fresh oregano, finely chopped

FOR THE SALAD
- Za'atar chickpeas (see above)
- 70g shredded white cabbage
- 30g chopped cavolo nero
- 100g yellow courgette, thinly sliced
- 60g cucumber, thinly sliced
- 60g green beans, steamed and halved
- 15g pickled chilli, chopped
- 40g pickled red onion (see above)
- 8–10 fresh mint leaves
- 15g flat-leaf parsley, chopped, plus extra to garnish
- 1 tsp sumac

## METHOD

**1.** Preheat the oven to 180°C fan (200°C/400°F). Toss the chickpeas with the za'atar, olive oil and a pinch of salt, then spread out on a baking tray. Roast for 10–12 minutes until golden and crisp. Let them cool completely, they'll go even crunchier as they sit.

**2.** While those are roasting, pickle the onion. Bring the vinegar, water, sugar and salt to the boil in a small pan. Add the sliced onion to a heatproof bowl or jar, then pour the hot liquid over the top. Let it sit for at least 1 hour until bright pink and punchy.

**3.** For the dressing, blitz the olive oil, lemon juice, mustard, salt, garlic and oregano in a blender until smooth and emulsified.

**4.** To assemble the salad, put the cooled chickpeas into a large bowl and toss with the cabbage, cavolo nero, courgette, cucumber, green beans, chopped pickled chilli, pickled red onion, mint and parsley. Season with a little salt, drizzle with the dressing and toss until everything's coated and glossy.

**5.** Scatter over a little extra parsley and the sumac and serve straight away. You can also let this sit in the fridge for a few hours – it gets even better once everything's had a chance to mingle.

# Nitai's Schug (A Family Recipe)

Ve / GF / DF

This is Nitai's family recipe, an old-school Yemeni-style schug that's been passed down through generations, and honestly, we're just lucky he's chosen to share it with us. It's fresh, fiery, herby, and punchy as hell, the kind of thing you end up spooning on to absolutely everything. Roasted veg? Add schug. Lamb kofta? Add schug. Mixed into yoghurt or tahini? Divine. Even scrambled eggs come alive with a drizzle of this green fire.

It's not about creating something unbearably hot, it's about building layers of flavour with herbs, garlic, spice and chilli. The texture should be loose and rustic, more like a coarse salsa than a smooth paste. If you've got a spice grinder, use it. If not, a food processor works, just don't blend in the oil or you'll lose the colour and vibrancy. Stir it through at the end.

**MAKES 1 LARGE JAR**
**PREP TIME: 20 MINS**

### INGREDIENTS

- 500g coriander
- 200g parsley
- 8-10 garlic cloves
- 5-15 green chillies, deseeded (to taste)
- 2 dried bird's eye chillies deseeded (or similar hot dry chillies)
- 3 cardamom pods
- 2 whole cloves
- 50ml extra virgin olive oil
- Sea salt and black pepper

FOR THE SPICES

- 15g fenugreek seeds or Amba Spice Blend (page 69)
- 15g cumin seeds
- 15g coriander seeds
- 20g ground cumin
- (or use 2 tbsp shop-bought baharat to replace all the above spices)

### METHOD

**1.** Start by washing your coriander and parsley thoroughly, then pat dry with a clean tea towel. You don't want soggy schug. Roughly chop the herbs and green chillies: this makes the blending or grinding process easier later on.

**2.** If using whole spices, toast the fenugreek, cumin and coriander seeds in a dry pan over a medium heat for 1-2 minutes until they smell amazing. Don't burn them. If using shop-bought baharat, skip this toasting step.

**3.** Combine the chopped herbs, chillies, garlic, toasted spices and ground cumin, or the baharat, cardamom pods, cloves and a generous pinch of salt and pepper in a food processor or spice grinder and pulse or grind until you get a coarse, loose paste: it should be chunky and full of texture. Taste it. You want it spicy, but not insane. The flavours will mellow a little as it sits, so don't be shy.

**4.** Once blended, gently stir in the olive oil by hand. Don't add the oil to the processor, or it will become a murky emulsified paste. You want the schug to stay bright and loose. Store in an airtight container in the fridge for up to 2 weeks.

# Za'atar Cauli Schnitzel, Caper Mayo + Schug

V / DF

Yes, we have tried to convince our kids these were chicken nuggets. Worked on one out of three. But honestly, once they dipped a crispy, golden cauli steak into that caper mayo, even the sceptics came round. This one's crunchy, comforting, and full of flavour, but if you skip the dips, it's pretty kid-friendly too (especially if you've got fussy ones like mine). And for us grown-ups, it hits that perfect spot, indulgent and satisfying like a plate of nuggets, but with the bonus of veg and two cracking dips to take it somewhere special.

**SERVES 4**
**PREP TIME: 20 MINS**
**COOK TIME: 20 MINS**

## INGREDIENTS
- 1 medium-large cauliflower (with leaves)
- 120g plain flour
- 3 eggs, beaten
- 150g breadcrumbs
- 1½ tbsp za'atar spice blend
- Vegetable oil, for shallow frying
- Sea salt and black pepper
- Lemon wedges, to serve
- Nitai's Schug (optional but brilliant; page 63), to serve

FOR THE CAPER MAYO
- 2 tbsp mayonnaise
- 1 tbsp capers, roughly chopped
- 1 small pickled cucumber or gherkin, roughly chopped
- Juice of ½ lemon

## METHOD

**1.** Start by mixing the caper mayo. Stir the chopped capers, pickle and lemon juice into the mayo and season with salt and pepper. Done. For the schug see recipe below.

**2.** Now for the schnitz. Trim the outer stems from the cauliflower but keep the smaller leaves – they go nice and crispy. Cut the cauliflower into steaks (about 3cm thick) and keep any florets that fall off.

**3.** Set up your breading station: one bowl with flour, one with beaten eggs, one with the breadcrumbs mixed with za'atar, salt and pepper. Dip each cauli steak into the flour, then the egg, then the za'atar breadcrumbs, pressing them on so everything sticks well. Do the same with the loose florets – you don't want to waste a single crumb.

**4.** Heat a good layer of oil in a large frying pan over a medium-high heat. Once hot, fry the schnitzels for 5-6 minutes on each side, or until golden and crisp. Drain on kitchen paper and keep going until they're all cooked.

**5.** Sprinkle with sea salt, serve with lemon wedges, caper mayo and schug.

ZA'ATAR

# Za'atar Smashed Cucumber Salad

Ve / GF / DF

This is one of those salads that somehow manages to be punchy, cooling, herby, and a bit addictive all at once. The cucumbers get smashed, literally, so they soak up all that lemony, za'atar-spiked dressing. It works brilliantly alongside anything hot off the grill or just eaten straight from the bowl when no one's looking. A bit of feta crumbled on top will take this somewhere else.

**SERVES 4–6 AS A SIDE**
**PREP TIME: 10 MINS**

## INGREDIENTS

- 2 large (or 4 small) cucumbers
- 1 garlic clove, grated
- 1–2 tsp za'atar spice blend (or to taste)
- 1 tbsp fresh oregano leaves, chopped (use fresh za'atar leaves if you can find them)
- 2 tbsp lemon juice
- 2 tbsp olive oil
- 1 tsp toasted sesame oil
- ½ tsp chilli flakes (optional, but great for a little heat)
- Handful of fresh parsley, chopped
- Handful of fresh mint, chopped (optional)
- 2 tbsp sesame seeds (mix of black and white), toasted
- Sea salt and black pepper

## METHOD

**1.** Lay the cucumbers on a chopping board and give them a good whack with the side of a big knife, wooden spoon or rolling pin – enough to crack them open without smashing them to mush. Slice into rough chunks and toss into a large bowl. Add the grated garlic, za'atar spice, chopped oregano or za'atar leaves, lemon juice, olive oil, sesame oil and chilli flakes (if using). Season generously with salt and pepper, then toss gently to coat everything evenly.

**2.** Add the parsley and mint (if using) and give the salad another light toss. Finish with a scatter of sesame seeds. Serve chilled or at room temperature.

# Amba

*a bit of Middle Eastern magic*

---

Amba might sound like a character from a children's book, but it's actually a punchy, fermented mango condiment that's a bit of a cult favourite at Farmer J. Beloved across the Middle East, it's traditionally made from green mangoes left to ferment with turmeric, fenugreek, mustard seeds, chilli and vinegar. The result is a sharp, sour, slightly funky sauce that packs heat, tang and fruit all in one go. It's like curry powder's more exciting cousin went backpacking and came home with stories.

It's earthy, citrusy and properly complex, and works like magic on roasted veg, grilled meats and in yoghurt. You'll taste cumin, mustard, maybe a bit of fenugreek and coriander in there – it's a bit hard to pin down, but that's what makes it so good.

# Amba Marinade

Ve / DF

The backbone of bold. This stuff's tangy, sweet and utterly addictive. Packed with warm Middle Eastern spices, garlic, soy, and a hit of date molasses to round it all out. It uses two spice blends: hawaij, an aromatic blend, and amba, a sour and dry blend. You can find these online or in specialist shops or make your own versions (see below).

**MAKES ABOUT 500ML**
**PREP TIME: 5 MINS**

**INGREDIENTS**
- 50g date molasses
- 15g garlic purée
- 25g hawaij spice blend (or see below)
- 7g ginger purée
- 50g amba spice blend (or see below)
- 125ml soy sauce
- 150ml neutral oil (such as avocado, pomace or sunflower oil)
- 5g onion granules
- 5g garlic granules
- 7g salt
- 5g coriander seeds
- 2.5g cumin seeds
- 2.5g black pepper

**METHOD**

**1.** Throw everything into a blender and blitz until totally smooth and emulsified. Pour into a jar or tub, seal tight and stick it in the fridge.

**2.** This will keep for a week in the fridge but it also freezes well if you've made a big batch.

## HAWAIJ SPICE BLEND
- 2 tbsp ground cumin
- 1 tbsp ground coriander
- 1 tbsp ground turmeric
- 1 tsp ground black pepper
- 1 tsp ground cardamom
- ½ tsp ground cloves
- ½ tsp ground cinnamon

## AMBA SPICE BLEND
- 2 tbsp ground fenugreek
- 2 tbsp ground turmeric
- 2 tbsp mango powder (amchur) – key for the sour tang
- 1 tbsp yellow mustard powder
- 1 tbsp garlic granules
- 1 tsp ground cumin
- 1 tsp ground coriander
- ½ tsp ground chilli (adjust to taste)

# Amba Chicken Thighs
DF

If you're only going to marinate one thing this week, make it this. These juicy, deeply spiced chicken thighs soak up every bit of the amba's sweet, tangy, garlicky punch. Char them, roast them, pan-fry them – just don't skip the resting time at the end.

**SERVES 4**
**PREP TIME: 10 MINS (PLUS MARINATING)**
**COOK TIME: 20–25 MINS**

## INGREDIENTS
- 1kg boneless, skinless chicken thighs
- 200g (or enough to coat generously) Amba Marinade (page 69)
- A splash of olive oil
- Salt, if needed (taste your marinade first)

TO SERVE
- Classic Tahini Sauce (page 83)
- Chopped fresh parsley
- Nitai's Schug (optional; page 63)

## METHOD

**1.** Get the chicken in a bowl or tub, pour over the amba marinade and rub it in like you really mean it. Every bit should be coated. Cover and chill for at least 4 hours, overnight if you've got the time. Pull the chicken out of the fridge 20–30 minutes before cooking so it's not fridge-cold when it hits the heat.

**2.** To grill: preheat the grill to medium-high and grill for 5–6 minutes on each side until charred and cooked through.

**3.** To pan-fry: place a large frying pan over a medium-high heat, add a splash of oil and cook for 5–7 minutes on each side until golden and caramelised.

**4.** To roast: preheat the oven to 200°C fan (220°C/425°F). Arrange the thighs in a roasting tray and roast for 20–25 minutes until cooked through and the juices run clear. The internal temperature should hit 75°C (165°F) on a probe thermometer.

**5.** However you've cooked your chicken, let it rest for 5 minutes before slicing or serving. Always. No one likes dry chicken.

**6.** Drizzle with Classic Tahini Sauce, a scatter of parsley, and a spoon of schug if you're into a bit of heat. Serve with rice, flatbread, grilled veg – whatever's going.

# Roasted Jerusalem Artichokes + Tahini-Amba Yoghurt

V / GF

These simple roasted Jerusalem artichokes were one of the first dishes Nitai ever made at Farmer J; from that moment, we knew we'd be a great team. It was seriously good – the kind of dish that makes people fall in love with vegetables. Crispy, golden Jerusalem artichokes (the knobbly little weirdos that roast like a dream), spooned over a yoghurt-tahini sauce that's been hit with amba spice, then finished with harissa oil and toasted almonds. Creamy, crunchy, spiced . . . yum.

**SERVES 4 AS A SIDE**
**PREP TIME: 15 MINS**
**COOK TIME: 45 MINS**

### INGREDIENTS
- 500g Jerusalem artichokes, scrubbed and halved
- 2 tbsp olive oil
- 3 garlic cloves, crushed
- 4 sprigs of thyme, leaves picked
- Zest of 1 lemon
- Sea salt and black pepper

FOR THE TAHINI-AMBA YOGHURT
- 200g Greek yoghurt
- 50g tahini
- 1 tbsp lemon juice
- 1 tbsp olive oil
- 1 small garlic clove, grated
- 1 tbsp Amba Spice Blend (page 69)

TO FINISH
- 1–2 tbsp harissa oil (or 1 tbsp harissa spice powder, mixed with 1–2 tbsp oil)
- Extra virgin olive oil, for drizzling
- Small handful of dill, finely chopped
- Small handful of parsley, finely chopped
- 30g toasted almonds, roughly chopped

### METHOD

**1.** Start by blanching the artichokes. Pop them into a saucepan, cover with cold water and add a big pinch of salt. Bring to the boil, then simmer gently for about 10 minutes until just tender, but not falling apart. Drain well and let them steam dry.

**2.** Preheat the oven to 180°C fan (200°C/400°F). Toss the blanched artichokes with the olive oil, garlic, thyme leaves and lemon zest and season with salt and pepper. Spread them out on a baking tray and roast for 25–30 minutes, flipping halfway, until they're golden and crisp on the edges.

**3.** While they roast, make the tahini-amba yoghurt. In a bowl, whisk together the yoghurt, tahini, lemon juice, olive oil, garlic and a pinch of salt until smooth. Stir in the amba spice. Taste and adjust the seasoning: it should be creamy, zippy, herby and have a gentle punch of spice. Chill until ready to serve.

**4.** To plate, smear the tahini-amba yoghurt on to the base of a serving platter. Pile the roasted artichokes on top. Drizzle with harissa oil and finish with a drizzle of extra virgin olive oil. Pile the herbs and almonds to one side. Serve warm or at room temperature, preferably with a hunk of good bread to mop up the sauce.

AMBA

# Leek + Chicken Kofta + Tzatziki

We love a good kofta, and these ones are a proper winner. Sweet caramelised leeks are folded into juicy ground chicken that is spiced with amba and held together with matzo meal. You can bake or fry them, and they're brilliant cold too. We serve them with a cooling tzatziki. But no one would stop at one: there are about five per person.

**SERVES 4–6 (MAKES ABOUT 26 KOFTAS)**
**PREP TIME: 30 MINS (PLUS CHILLING)**
**COOK TIME: 25-30 MINS**

### INGREDIENTS
- 1kg leeks
- 50ml olive oil
- 500g chicken mince
- 150–200g matzo meal or panko breadcrumbs
- 2 eggs
- 2 tbsp Amba Spice Blend (page 69)
- 1 garlic clove, grated
- Sea salt and black pepper
- Lemon wedges, to serve
- A few sprigs of dill, to garnish

FOR THE TZATZIKI
- 150g Greek yoghurt
- 1 garlic clove, grated
- 1 cucumber, grated and squeezed dry
- Small handful each of dill and mint, finely chopped
- 1 olive oil

### METHOD
**1.** Clean the leeks thoroughly and slice them into half-moons. Sauté in the olive oil over a medium-low heat until soft and golden, about 20 minutes. You will need a big pan to fit them all in but the leeks cook down significantly, so be patient! Lift out of the pan, draining any excess olive oil, and cool completely.

**2.** Mix the cooled leeks with the chicken, matzo meal, eggs, amba spice, garlic, salt and pepper. Get in there with your hands and mix it all up. It's a wet mixture but the matzo/breadcrumbs will soak up some of the moisture. Chill for 30 minutes or ideally overnight to firm up.

**3.** Preheat the oven to 220°C fan (240°C/465°F). Shape the mix into small patties or balls and lay on a lined tray. Drizzle with oil and bake for 15–20 minutes until golden. Alternatively, pan-fry in a little oil over a medium-high heat until crisp on both sides.

**4.** While they're cooking, mix all the ingredients for the tzatziki in a bowl, then season to taste with salt and pepper.

**5.** Serve the hot kofta with a big dollop of the cold tzatziki. Add lemon wedges for squeezing and a few sprigs of dill. Perfect for any day that needs a little spice.

AMBA

# Stuffed Spiced Pitta + Alice's Yoghurt Leeks

Picture this: a balmy summer evening, the scent of spiced meat wafting from the grill, and hands reaching eagerly for these golden, stuffed pitta pockets. Brimming with Middle Eastern warmth and a touch of rustic charm, this recipe is as comforting as it is easy.

Alice is Farmer J's incredible Commercial Director, who also happens to be my best friend. We've worked together, travelled together, cooked together, laughed and cried together (often in the same meeting) and somehow still like each other enough to share a kitchen. The yoghurt leeks dish is rooted in Alice's Turkish heritage and is deceptively simple: just leeks, yoghurt and spice, but the result is magic: a lush, silky, almost dip-like dish that works with everything.
(Main image overleaf, with Tommy's Freekancini (page 201) and Kalamata Gilda (page 167) at top left.)

**SERVES 4**
**PREP TIME: 20 MINS**
**COOK TIME: 25 MINS**

### INGREDIENTS
- 500g beef mince (ideally 20% fat)
- 1 onion, finely chopped
- 15g pine nuts, toasted and chopped
- 15g pistachios, toasted and chopped
- 1 tbsp harissa paste (page 39, or shop-bought)
- 1 tsp sweet paprika
- 1 garlic clove, finely chopped
- 10g Amba Spice Blend (page 69, or use curry powder)
- 10g Preserved Lemon (page 175), chopped
- Generous pinch of sea salt
- A splash of sparkling water
- 2 medium-sized pittas

FOR THE YOGHURT LEEKS
- 400g leeks, cut into rounds
- Knob of unsalted butter
- Extra virgin olive oil
- 150g full-fat Greek-style yoghurt
- 1 tbsp pul biber (Turkish chilli flakes, also known as Aleppo pepper)
- Sea salt and black pepper
- 1 tbsp sumac

TO SERVE
- Classic Tahini Sauce (page 83)
- Pickles
- Labneh (page 40)

## METHOD

**1.** Start by prepping your leeks. Remove any battered outer leaves, then slice each leek vertically down the middle, keeping the root end intact. Rinse under cold running water to get rid of any grit, then trim off the roots and dark green tops. Slice into 1cm thick rounds.

**2.** Melt the butter and a good glug of olive oil in a large frying pan over a low heat. Add the leeks and sauté slowly, stirring regularly, for 12–15 minutes. You want them soft, sweet and caramelised, not browned – low and slow is the way here.

**3.** Meanwhile, add the beef mince, onion, pine nuts, pistachios, harissa, paprika, garlic, amba, preserved lemon and salt to a large bowl. Use your hands to mix until everything is well distributed: don't be shy – get stuck in! Gradually add the sparkling water as you knead the mixture. This little secret keeps the meat wonderfully moist as it grills.

**4.** Slice the pittas in half to create pockets. Generously stuff each half with the spiced meat mixture, pressing it down gently to flatten the open side. This ensures even grilling and prevents it from spilling out.

**5.** Preheat your grill to 210°C fan (410°F) and place the filled pittas open-side down. Sear for a minute or two, then gently grill the sides over a medium heat until the bread is golden and slightly crisp, and the filling is cooked through.

**6.** Once the leeks are meltingly tender, turn off the heat. Stir in the Greek yoghurt, pul biber, and a good seasoning of salt and pepper. Sprinkle on some sumac to serve.

**7.** Serve your stuffed spiced pittas with the yoghurt leeks, and bowls of tahini, pickles and labneh.

# Condiments & Sauces

| Tahini | Miso | Date Molasses | Yeast Extract |
|:---:|:---:|:---:|:---:|
| *82* | *96* | *104* | *114* |

# Tahini

*the sauce that does it all*

---

There was a moment – a dark, terrifying moment – when we thought Ali was allergic to tahini. Nitai had a full-blown panic attack, Jonathan was ready to file for divorce, and Ali wanted to cry. Because let's be real, we use tahini in almost everything at Farmer J. The idea of a tahini-free life was unthinkable. Don't panic, Ali's fine. But let's just say it reaffirmed what we already knew: tahini isn't just an ingredient; it's the backbone of half the things we love.

There's something a bit magical about tahini. One spoon of the stuff and suddenly you've got depth, richness, nuttiness – it somehow manages to be creamy and punchy all at once. Made from nothing more than sesame seeds, it's the kind of ingredient that can go from classic falafel dressing to French beurre blanc without breaking a sweat. We throw it on everything, and once you start using it, you'll be doing the same.

Here's a fun fact: it takes a whole kilogram of sesame seeds to make just 200g of tahini. So yes, it's precious, but it's worth it. That spoonful might not look like much, but the impact is massive, adding body, richness and a bit of flair to whatever it touches.

We use tahini every way we can think of, so as well as our Classic Tahini Sauce you'll find Spicy Green Tahini, our go-to for zingy veg or grilled meats. We've even got Chocolate Tahini – try it on ice cream or porridge and thank us later.

The bottom line? Tahini's a kitchen workhorse dressed like a star.

# Classic Tahini Sauce

Ve / GF / DF

This is the sauce we reach for again and again. It's creamy, nutty, lemony, and just works with everything: drizzled on roast veg, spooned over grain bowls, mopped up with warm pitta, or thinned out into a dressing. No chilli, no herbs, just proper classic tahini flavour done right.

**MAKES 700–800G**
**PREP TIME: 10 MINS**

### INGREDIENTS
- 1 small garlic clove, chopped
- 1 tsp sea salt
- Juice of 1 large lemon
- 50ml olive oil
- 150ml room-temperature water
- 500g raw tahini
- 250ml ice-cold water

### METHOD

**1.** Start by blending the garlic, salt, lemon juice, olive oil and room-temperature water in a food processor or blender until smooth. It'll look thin and a bit pale, but that's perfect. Add the tahini and blend again. It'll thicken quickly, then loosen as it blends – don't panic, just keep going. Slowly add the ice-cold water a little at a time until the sauce is silky, smooth and pourable. Taste and adjust – more lemon if you want it zingier, more salt if it needs a lift.

**2.** Store in an airtight jar in the fridge for up to a week. If it thickens up, just stir in a splash of water before serving. Shake, drizzle, dip, repeat.

# Spicy Green Tahini

Ve / GF / DF

This one's a proper Farmer J staple. It's punchy and herby and has just the right amount of kick. The pickled chilli brings heat without blowing your head off, and the parsley gives it that fresh, grassy edge.

**MAKES ABOUT 700G**
**PREP TIME: 10 MINS**

### INGREDIENTS
- ½ tsp sea salt
- 1 small garlic clove, chopped
- 3½ tbsp (or more to taste) pickled green chillies
- 50g fresh parsley, chopped
- 50ml lemon juice (about 1 large lemon)
- 50ml olive oil
- 150ml pickled chilli water (from the chilli jar)
- 250ml ice-cold water
- 500g tahini

### METHOD

**1.** In a blender or food processor, combine the salt, garlic, pickled chillies, parsley, lemon juice, olive oil, pickle water and ice-cold water. Blitz until you've got a thin, bright green base – it should be smooth but still fresh-looking.

**2.** Add the tahini and blend again until the whole thing comes together into a thick, creamy, pourable sauce. If it looks too thick, just add a splash more ice-cold water or lemon juice until you hit the right texture.

**3.** Taste and tweak with more salt, lemon or chilli. Store in an airtight jar in the fridge for up to a week. Shake well before using and pour generously.

# Burnt Aubergine, Tahini + Pistachios

Ve / GF / DF

Smoky, nutty, creamy, tangy: this dish somehow manages to be all things at once. We love it as part of a mezze spread, but it holds its own beautifully alongside grilled meat, or with a warm flatbread to scoop it all up. It heroes raw tahini, gets a punch of sweetness from the date molasses, and yes, trust us on those raspberries – they bring a little zingy surprise that absolutely works.

**SERVES 2–4 AS A SIDE**
**PREP TIME: 30 MINS**
**COOK TIME: 10–20 MINS**

### INGREDIENTS
- 1 large aubergine
- Juice of ½ lemon
- 50g raw tahini
- A good drizzle of date molasses
- 50g roasted pistachios, roughly chopped
- 30g pomegranate seeds
- 5-8 raspberries, some whole, some halved (blueberries make a good alternative)
- 2 tbsp Greek yoghurt (optional)
- Extra virgin olive oil
- Sea salt

### METHOD

**1.** Using tongs, char the aubergine directly over an open flame, gas hob or barbecue for 8-10 minutes, turning now and then until the skin is completely blackened and the inside feels soft and collapsing. No flame? Stick it under a hot grill for 15-20 minutes, turning a few times to get that same char. Once soft, let the aubergine cool in a sieve over a bowl. When it's cool enough to handle, peel away the skin with your hands or a spoon (don't worry about a few charred bits, they add flavour). Let the flesh drain for a few more minutes to get rid of the excess moisture.

**2.** Transfer the aubergine to a plate, and flatten with the side of a knife. You want a rustic, uneven layer (not too neat). Squeeze over the lemon juice and sprinkle with sea salt. Drizzle over the tahini and follow with the date molasses. Scatter over the pistachios, pomegranate seeds and raspberries (don't skip them, they cut through the richness beautifully). Dot with the yoghurt (if using) and finish with a glug of olive oil.

**3.** Eat with something to mop it up – pitta, flatbread, a spoon – anything goes.

TAHINI

# Whole Roast Celeriac + Celeriac + Tahini Cream

Ve (without butter) / GF / DF

This is one of those dishes that makes a usually underrated bit of veg feel wonderfully luxurious. We're big fans of celeriac at Farmer J; it's earthy and, when roasted whole, turns sweet, nutty and utterly delicious. We roast it until golden and soft, then serve it on a silky tahini and caramelised celeriac cream. Add some crunch and zing with nuts and chimichurri, and you've got a knockout centrepiece.

**SERVES 4**
**PREP TIME: 15 MINS**
**COOK TIME: 1½ HOURS**

### INGREDIENTS

FOR THE WHOLE ROASTED CELERIAC
- 1 whole celeriac, peeled
- Olive oil
- Sea salt and black pepper

FOR THE CARAMELISED CELERIAC AND TAHINI CREAM
- 1–2 tbsp olive oil
- Knob of butter (or use olive oil)
- 1 medium-large celeriac (600g), peeled and cubed into 2–3cm chunks
- 150ml milk (dairy or plant-based), or enough to cover
- 80g tahini
- Sea salt and white pepper

TO FINISH
- Chimichurri (page 00)
- Roasted almonds or hazelnuts, roughly chopped

### METHOD

**1.** Preheat the oven to 200°C fan (220°C/425°F). Peel your whole celeriac and give it a good rub with olive oil, salt and pepper. Wrap it tightly in baking parchment and then foil and roast on a tray for about 1 hour 15 minutes. You're aiming for soft, golden and slightly collapsed. Stick a fork in to check; if it slides in easily, you're there.

**2.** While that's roasting, get on with the caramelised celeriac cream. Heat the olive oil and butter (if using) in a pan over a medium-low heat, then chuck in the cubed celeriac. Ideally, use a pan that allows the celeriac to be in one layer. Cook gently, stirring now and then, until it's golden and caramelised all over – this'll take 20–25 minutes but is well worth your patience. Season with salt and white pepper.

**3.** Once it's got that rich colour, pour in enough milk to just cover it. Pop a lid on and simmer for 10–15 minutes until the celeriac is completely tender. Strain, reserving the liquid. Blend the celeriac until smooth, adding the cooking liquid a little at a time to loosen (add a little more milk if needed), then blend in the tahini until you've got a glossy, creamy purée. Taste and tweak the seasoning.

**4.** Once the whole roasted celeriac is done, unwrap it and either leave it whole or cut into wedges. Spoon a thick layer of the caramelised celeriac and tahini cream on to a plate. Top with the roasted celeriac, a drizzle of chimichurri and a good handful of roasted nuts for crunch. Serve warm with some good bread for mopping.

TAHINI

# Tuna, Green Bean + Raw Tahini Tartare

DF

This is one of those dishes that feels sophisticated but is deceptively simple. Just make sure you've got good-quality tuna – sashimi-grade is non-negotiable. And don't even think about making this ahead of time as it needs to be served fresh, straight from chopping board to plate. It's a creation from Shuli, one of our former (and much-loved) Heads of Food. We first tried it years ago and have been hooked ever since. Raw tahini with raw fish? Genius. Raw green beans with raw tahini and raw fish? Even better. Clean, rich, nutty, tahini brings the whole thing together.

**SERVES 2–4 AS A STARTER**
**PREP TIME: 15 MINS**

## INGREDIENTS

- 180g sashimi-grade tuna, cut into small cubes
- 50g raw green beans, finely chopped
- 1 small shallot, finely chopped
- 1 tbsp olive oil
- ¼ tsp chilli flakes (or to taste)
- 10g fresh coriander, finely chopped
- A good pinch of sea salt
- Small knob of ginger, peeled and finely chopped (optional)
- 1 tsp coriander seeds, crushed (optional)
- 1 tbsp raw tahini
- Zest of ½ lemon
- Pane carasau (or any decent cracker or flatbread)

## METHOD

**1.** Pop the tuna into a bowl with the finely chopped green beans and shallot. Drizzle over the olive oil, toss in the chilli flakes, chopped coriander and salt, plus the ginger and coriander seeds (if using). Give it a gentle stir, but don't bash it about – you need to treat it kindly.

**2.** Spoon on to a serving plate or into a shallow bowl. Drizzle over the raw tahini and finish with a good grating of lemon zest.

**3.** Serve straight away with sheets of pane carasau or your cracker of choice.

TAHINI

# Chocolate Tahini Tiramisu

V

Tiramisu, but with a tahini twist. This version ditches the delicate and dives straight into rich, earthy decadence. The chocolate tahini adds depth and nuttiness that plays off the coffee and cream like a dream. It's still layered, still luxurious, just with a darker, slightly rebellious edge. The kind of dessert that steals the show and silences the table.

**SERVES 4–6**
**PREP TIME: 30 MINS (PLUS CHILLING)**

## INGREDIENTS

FOR THE MASCARPONE CREAM
- 6 eggs, separated
- 160g caster sugar
- 800g mascarpone
- 1 vanilla pod (seeds scraped out) or 1 tsp vanilla extract (optional)
- Pinch of sea salt

FOR THE COFFEE INFUSION
- 10 espresso shots (or 120ml strong coffee)
- 100g maple syrup
- ½ tbsp baharat spice blend (optional)
- 60ml sweet fortified wine, such as Marsala or sweet sherry (optional)
- 20-24 ladyfinger biscuits (savoiardi)

FOR THE CHOCOLATE TAHINI MIX
- 150g Chocolate Tahini (or more if you're feeling decadent; page 93)
- 2-3 tbsp of the coffee infusion

TO DECORATE
- Dark cocoa powder or grated dark chocolate

## METHOD

**1.** Start with the mascarpone cream. Whisk the egg yolks with 120g of the sugar in a large bowl until the mixture turns pale and fluffy. Gradually add the mascarpone, along with the vanilla (if using) and a pinch of sea salt. Whisk until smooth, creamy and utterly luscious.

**2.** Tip the egg whites into a clean bowl and whisk using a hand-held electric whisk until frothy and doubled in size. Gradually add the remaining 40g sugar, a little at a time, and continue whisking until stiff peaks form (when the whites hold their shape firmly without collapsing).

**3.** Gently fold the whipped egg whites into the mascarpone mixture in three batches, using a silicone spatula to keep the mixture light and airy. For tiramisu, remember, always add the light to the heavy.

**4.** Now for the coffee infusion. Combine the espresso, maple syrup and baharat (if using) in a shallow dish and whisk until combined. If you'd like to add a boozy note, a splash of fortified wine would be delightful.

**5.** It's chocolate tahini time. In a separate bowl (it's the last bowl, I promise), mix the chocolate tahini with 2–3 tablespoons of the coffee infusion to loosen it to a smooth, spreadable consistency.

**6.** Now to the assembly. Quickly dip each ladyfinger into the coffee infusion, ensuring they soak up the liquid but don't become soggy – a quick 1–2 seconds is all it takes. Arrange a layer of the soaked ladyfingers in your chosen serving dish. Spread a generous layer of the chocolate tahini over the ladyfingers. Follow with a layer of the mascarpone cream, smoothing

it out with the back of a spoon. Repeat the layers: soaked ladyfingers, chocolate tahini, mascarpone cream. Depending on the size of your dish, you should have two or three layers. Finish with a final layer of mascarpone cream, smoothing the top.

**7.** Finally, dust the top with dark cocoa powder for that classic tiramisu finish or (my preference) finely grate dark chocolate over the top – be generous. Cover and refrigerate for at least 4 hours or overnight.

# Chocolate Tahini Challah Bread Pudding
V

Rich, nutty, gooey and just indulgent enough to make you close your eyes mid-bite. This is your standard bread pudding turned all the way up, thanks to chocolate tahini. Think of it as a grown-up chocolate spread swirl but deeper, earthier and far more sophisticated.

**SERVES 6–8**
**PREP TIME: 25 MINS**
**COOK TIME: 35 MINS**

## INGREDIENTS
FOR THE CHOCOLATE TAHINI
- 100g dark chocolate
- 30g cacao powder
- 120g tahini
- 30g maple syrup
- Pinch of sea salt
- ½ tsp vanilla extract
- 1 tbsp coconut oil (optional)

FOR THE BREAD PUDDING
- 4 eggs
- 400ml whole milk
- 200ml double cream
- 50g caster sugar
- 1 tsp vanilla extract
- Pinch of salt
- 75g Chocolate Tahini (see above)
- 400g challah, brioche or panettone torn or cubed (slightly stale is best)
- 50g dark chocolate chunks or chips (optional)
- Sesame seeds or chunks of halva, to finish
- Whipped cream or ice cream, to serve

## METHOD
**1.** First, make your chocolate tahini. Melt the dark chocolate in a small pan over a low heat or in the microwave. Remove from the heat and stir in the cacao powder. Whisk through the tahini, maple syrup, sea salt, vanilla extract and coconut oil (if using). Store in an airtight jar in the fridge for up to a week.

**2.** Preheat the oven to 170°C fan (190°C/375°F) and grease a baking dish (about 1.5 litre capacity) with butter.

**3.** Whisk the eggs, milk, cream, sugar, vanilla and salt in a bowl until smooth. Gently warm the chocolate tahini until pourable (microwave for 10–15 seconds), then whisk that in too.

**4.** Add the challah chunks to the baking dish and pour over the custard. Press down gently with your hands or a spatula so the bread gets good and soaked. Let it sit for 15 minutes. Scatter over dark chocolate chunks (if using). Bake for 30–35 minutes until just set, with a slight wobble in the middle.

**5.** Scatter sesame seeds or halva over the top and serve warm with whipped cream, ice cream, or just some spoons and a good excuse.

# Honey, Tahini + Olive Oil Bundt

V

This cake is pure alchemy: golden honey, nutty tahini and lush olive oil come together to create a tender, deeply flavoured sponge. Warm spices like cinnamon and baharat add intrigue, while a drizzle of date molasses and tahini over the top takes it to luxurious new heights. Best served with a strong cup of coffee and a dollop of crème fraîche.

**SERVES 10–12**
**PREP TIME: 20 MINS (PLUS COOLING)**
**COOKING TIME: 45–50 MINS**

### INGREDIENTS

- 3 large eggs
- 300g honey
- 30g date molasses, plus extra for drizzling
- 150ml olive oil, plus extra for greasing
- 200g caster sugar
- 30g raw tahini, plus extra for drizzling
- 1 tsp ground cinnamon
- 1 tsp baharat spice blend
- Pinch of sea salt
- 350g plain flour
- 2 tsp baking powder
- 240ml strong tea or coffee
- 50g toasted almond flakes, to decorate
- Crème fraîche, to serve (optional)

### METHOD

**1.** Preheat the oven to 180°C fan (200°C/400°F) and grease a 23cm bundt cake tin with olive oil.

**2.** In a large bowl, whisk together the eggs, honey, date molasses and olive oil until smooth and glossy. Add the sugar and mix until fully combined.

**3.** Stir in the raw tahini, cinnamon, baharat and a good pinch of sea salt. The mixture should smell warm and inviting. Sift in the flour and baking powder in two stages, folding gently to keep it light. Gradually pour in the tea or coffee (whichever you prefer), stirring until the batter is smooth and pourable – it should flow like thick honey.

**4.** Pour the batter into the prepared tin and smooth the top. Slide the cake into the oven and immediately reduce the temperature to 160°C fan (180°C/350°F). This helps the cake bake slowly and evenly, giving you that signature moist crumb.

**5.** Bake for 45–50 minutes, or until a skewer poked into the centre comes out clean. If it's browning too quickly and not yet cooked, cover with a sheet of foil to prevent burning. The top should be golden and your kitchen should smell insane.

**6.** Let it cool in the tin for 15–20 minutes before carefully turning out on to a wire rack to cool completely. While the cake is still warm, drizzle over more date molasses and raw tahini. Scatter toasted almond flakes on top for a bit of crunch. Serve with crème fraîche, if you like.

TAHINI

95

# Miso

*deeply savoury, always delicious*

---

There's something quietly powerful about miso. Made from soybeans, rice or barley and a whole lot of patience, miso is a fermented paste that's been around for thousands of years. It's salty, packed with umami and has this deep, fermented funk that transforms whatever it touches.

At Farmer J, miso is one of those ingredients we always have knocking about. It's the kind of thing you didn't realise you were missing until you started using it; then suddenly it's in everything. We whisk it into dressings, stir it through marinades and rub it on veg. It adds a kind of savoury backbone, a richness that doesn't scream for attention but gives the whole dish a bit more guts. Just a spoonful is enough to take something from bland to bold.

It's brilliant on veg, especially the ones that get a bad rap. Take your Christmas sprouts, slap them with a miso dressing, roast until crispy and caramelised, and suddenly no one's complaining. It does wonders with aubergine too, turning that creamy flesh into something smoky, sweet and salty all at once.

We're not saying miso is a miracle but we're also not not saying that. It's plant-based, lasts for ever in the fridge and never lets you down. Basically, it's the quiet hero of the kitchen.

# Miso Dressing

Ve / GF / DF

This is one of those dressings we keep coming back to: sweet, salty, zingy and properly umami. We use white miso for its mellow, buttery sweetness, but any miso will do the job. Just whisk, taste and pour it on thick. Goes with just about everything.

**MAKES ABOUT 600ML**
**PREP TIME: 5–10 MINS**

### INGREDIENTS
- 290g white miso
- 200ml rice vinegar
- 50ml mirin
- 180ml avocado or pomace oil
- 40ml toasted sesame oil
- 30g fresh ginger, peeled and grated
- 1 tbsp dark brown sugar

### METHOD

**1.** Add the miso, rice vinegar and mirin to a large bowl and whisk until smooth – no lumpy bits allowed. Slowly drizzle in half of the avocado oil while whisking, then drizzle in the sesame oil. Add the ginger and stir through the sugar until fully dissolved. It should start to smell incredible.

**2.** Now add the remaining avocado oil, slowly whisking the whole time until the dressing turns silky and glossy.

**3.** Taste and tweak: add more sugar if you want it sweeter, more vinegar if you're after a bigger punch.

**4.** Use it straight away or stash it in the fridge in a sealed jar. It'll keep for up to 2 weeks; just give it a shake before serving.

# A Lot of Mushrooms + Miso Dressing

V / GF (use gluten-free soy sauce) / DF (without butter)

If you're a mushroom lover, this one's going to hit hard. It's deeply savoury, full of texture and properly indulgent with that sticky miso glaze. The soy-cured egg yolk is the rich, salty crown on top: soft, golden and ready to be stirred through. Serve with toast, rice, or just a spoon and a bit of quiet.

**SERVES 4 AS A SIDE OR 2 AS A MAIN**
**PREP TIME: 15 MINS (PLUS CURING)**
**COOK TIME: 15 MINS**

### INGREDIENTS
- 100g oyster mushrooms
- 100g king oyster mushrooms
- 100g portobello mushrooms
- 100g girolles (chanterelles)
- 100g shimeji mushrooms
- Olive oil or butter, for cooking
- 2–3 sprigs of thyme, leaves picked and stems discarded
- 100ml rice wine
- 100ml Miso Dressing (page 97)
- Handful of chives, finely chopped

FOR THE SOY-CURED EGG YOLK
- 120ml soy sauce
- 2 tbsp mirin
- 4 free-range egg yolks

### METHOD

**1.** Start by curing the egg yolks. Mix the soy sauce and mirin in a small bowl and gently lower in the yolks (keep the whites for another dish). Chill for 4–8 hours, or overnight if you're planning ahead. They'll firm up and soak in all that salty-sweet goodness.

**2.** Clean your mushrooms by wiping gently with a damp cloth: no rinsing or they'll become slimy. Slice the oyster, king oyster and portobello into bite-sized bits. Leave the girolles and shimeji mostly whole or tear them up a little.

**3.** Heat a large pan over a medium heat and add a splash of olive oil or a knob of butter. Add all the mushrooms and sauté for about 7 minutes, stirring now and then, until they start to soften and brown. Add the thyme, then pour in the rice wine and let it bubble down for a minute or two until most of the liquid's gone. Now add the miso dressing and cook for another few minutes, stirring so it clings to every mushroom and caramelises just slightly. It should smell outrageous by this point.

**4.** Spoon the mushrooms on to a serving plate and carefully place a soy-cured yolk on top. Finish with a generous scattering of chives and serve straight away. Break the yolk and let its rich silkiness tie the whole dish together.

# Roasted Brussels Sprouts + Hispi + Miso-Maple-Tahini

Ve / GF / DF

This dish has earned its place at our Farmer J Christmas table and frankly, it turns up throughout November too. It's the one that converts sprout-haters into sprout-lovers. We've lost count of how many people have said: 'Wait, sprouts are actually good?' Yes, yes they are. Especially when you roast them until crispy, pair them with charred hispi, and drown the whole lot in our miso-maple-tahini dressing. Creamy, salty, sweet, nutty – it's got it all.

**SERVES 4 AS A SIDE**
**PREP TIME: 15 MINS**
**COOK TIME: 30 MINS**

### INGREDIENTS

- 300g Brussels sprouts, halved
- 200g hispi cabbage, cut into wedges
- 2 tbsp olive oil
- 100ml Miso Dressing (page 97)
- 1 tbsp toasted sesame seeds
- Small handful of fresh coriander, finely chopped
- Sea salt and black pepper

FOR THE MISO-MAPLE-TAHINI DRESSING
- 50ml Miso Dressing (from the 100ml above) (page 97)
- 50ml maple syrup
- 150g tahini
- 20ml rice vinegar
- 3–4 tbsp water, to loosen
- 1 tbsp toasted sesame oil

### METHOD

**1.** Preheat the oven to 180°C fan (200°C/400°F) and line a roasting tray with baking parchment.

**2.** Toss the halved sprouts and hispi wedges into a bowl with the olive oil, half of the miso dressing and a good pinch of salt and pepper. Spread them out on the lined tray (don't crowd them) and roast for 25–30 minutes, flipping halfway, until golden and catching at the edges.

**3.** While the veg are roasting, make the dressing. Whisk together the miso dressing, maple syrup and tahini until smooth. Stir in the rice vinegar, then slowly add the water until creamy but pourable. Finish with the sesame oil.

**4.** Toss the roasted veg into a bowl with the remaining 50ml of the miso dressing to coat them while they're hot and ready to soak it all up. Pile on to a serving platter and drizzle generously with the miso-maple-tahini dressing. Finish with toasted sesame seeds or a scatter of chopped herbs. Serve warm and prepare to be told you've changed someone's mind about sprouts.

### Tip

You can swap the Brussels sprouts for aubergine if you're making this outside sprout season. Just cut 1 large or 2 medium aubergines into thick wedges or chunks. Roast them the same way: toss in oil and miso dressing, spread out on a tray, and cook until golden and soft with crispy edges. They soak up the miso-maple-tahini like a dream.

# Kale Miso Slaw

Ve / GF / DF

This one's a proper Farmer J classic. It's been on the menu for as long as we can remember and it's never coming off – people love it too much. It's crunchy, punchy, zingy, sweet, savoury . . . the whole lot. The quick-pickled cabbage brings the bite and the creamy miso dressing pulls everything together. And the kale? Just make sure you give it a good massage; we want none of that raw, scratchy nonsense here. Once it's softened up, it drinks in the flavour like a dream.

**SERVES 4–6**
**PREP TIME: 20 MINS (PLUS PICKLING)**

**INGREDIENTS**
FOR THE QUICK-PICKLED RED CABBAGE
- 600ml cold water
- 250ml apple cider vinegar
- 50g soft light brown sugar
- 10g sea salt
- 5g black peppercorns
- 5g coriander seeds, toasted
- Small bunch (about 25g) of dill
- 1kg red cabbage, shredded

FOR THE SWEET WHITE MISO DRESSING
- 1 heaped tbsp sweet white miso
- 1 tbsp rice vinegar
- 1cm piece of fresh ginger, peeled and finely chopped
- 2 tbsp sunflower oil
- 1 tbsp toasted sesame oil
- 1 tbsp tamari
- 2 tsp maple syrup

FOR THE SLAW
- 200g kale, stalks removed, leaves washed and shredded
- 200g white cabbage, shredded
- 8 radishes, thinly sliced
- 200g pickled red cabbage (see above)
- 1 ripe avocado, sliced and dressed with lemon juice
- 2 tsp black and white sesame seeds, toasted
- 50g roasted cashews, roughly chopped

**METHOD**

**1.** Start with the pickled cabbage. In a big clean tub or jar, stir together the water, vinegar, sugar, salt, peppercorns, toasted coriander seeds and dill until the sugar has dissolved. Add the shredded red cabbage and press down so it's fully submerged. Pop the lid on, then stick it in the fridge for 24 hours. You'll have more than you need for the slaw but it keeps well for up to 2 weeks.

**2.** Now make the dressing. Whisk all the ingredients together in a bowl until smooth and creamy.

**3.** To make the slaw, throw the kale, white cabbage, sliced radishes and a handful of your pickled cabbage into a large bowl. Pour over half the dressing and give it a good massage. You need to really get your hands in there and work it until the kale softens and goes glossy.

**4.** Pile it into a serving dish, top with the avocado, scatter over your sesame seeds and cashews, then finish with the rest of the dressing. Big flavour, big crunch, and good for you.

MISO

# Roasted Tofu, Hispi + Aubergine + Smoked Chilli Miso

Ve / GF / DF

The kind of dinner that feels like a hug but still gives you enough fire to wake up your taste buds. We make it with our smoky chilli miso sauce - punchy, rich and with a subtle sweetness that balances beautifully with roasted aubergine, crispy tofu and those caramelised chunks of hispi. We make this at Farmer J all winter long; honestly, we never get bored of it.

**SERVES 4**
**PREP TIME: 20 MINS**
**COOK TIME: 35-40 MINS**

### INGREDIENTS
- 400g firm tofu, cut into 3-4 cm cubes
- 1 hispi cabbage, cut into 6-8 chunky wedges (depending on the size of the cabbage)
- 1 aubergine, cut into 3-4cm chunks
- Neutral oil (such as avocado, pomace or sunflower oil)
- 150ml coconut milk
- Rice, to serve

FOR THE SMOKED CHILLI MISO SAUCE
- 3-4 smoked dried chillies (chipotle, guajillo or pasilla)
- 200g white or red miso
- 2 tbsp rice vinegar
- 1 tbsp soy sauce
- 1 tbsp maple syrup or soft dark brown sugar
- 1 tbsp toasted sesame oil
- 20g fresh ginger, peeled and grated
- 2 garlic cloves, grated
- 50g rice wine or mirin
- 3-4 tbsp water

TO FINISH
- Chives or spring onions, thinly sliced
- Toasted sesame seeds
- Big handful of fresh coriander

### METHOD

**1.** First, make the smoked chilli miso sauce. Deseed the dried chillies and soak them in warm water for 10-15 minutes until soft, then remove the stems and seeds. Chuck them into a blender with all the remaining sauce ingredients and blitz until smooth. Add more water if needed to loosen it up. Set aside.

**2.** Preheat the oven to 200°C fan (220°C/425°F) and line three baking trays with baking parchment. Toss the tofu cubes into a bowl with about 4-5 tablespoons of the smoked chilli miso sauce to give them a good coating. Spread them out on a lined tray. Toss the cabbage and the aubergine separately with some of the same sauce and a little oil and place on separate trays. Roast the aubergine and tofu for 25 minutes until both are caramelised and tender. Add the tray of cabbage for the final 10 minutes.

**3.** Get a large cast-iron or ovenproof dish and layer the roasted cabbage in the base. Spoon the tofu over the top, then the roasted aubergine. In a small bowl, mix most of the remaining miso sauce (reserve 1-2 tablespoons to finish the dish) with the coconut milk, stir well, then pour it over the dish, letting it coat everything. Crank the oven temperature up to 230°C fan (250°C/480°F) and roast for 10-12 minutes until it's bubbling and starting to char in places.

**4.** To finish, drizzle over a little more of the smoked chilli miso sauce, then hit it with spring onions, sesame seeds and a proper handful of chopped coriander. Serve straight from the pan with rice.

# Date Molasses

*always a good idea*

---

There's a reason we're obsessed with date molasses at Farmer J. This sticky, dark syrup is made by slowly reducing dates until they give up all their natural sweetness and depth, leaving behind a thick, rich molasses that tastes like treacle's cooler cousin. It's been a staple across the Middle East and North Africa for centuries, used in everything from marinades to pastries. And once you get your hands on it, you'll never look at honey or maple syrup the same way again.

We love it for its versatility. It brings a dark caramel sweetness with hints of toffee, but it's also got this slightly savoury tang that makes it perfect in both sweet and savoury dishes. You can slather it over porridge or pancakes in the morning, whisk it into a vinaigrette for roasted roots, or mix it into a glaze for slow-cooked chicken or lamb that'll make your kitchen smell like something special is happening (because it is). It's also magic when stirred into a yoghurt bowl or baked into a cake. Basically, it's a good idea whatever direction you take it.

# Smashed Sweet Potatoes + Date Molasses Tahini + Crispy Onions

Ve, DF (can be GF if cornflour or GF flour is used)

Roasted sweet potatoes, smashed and crisped until golden and caramelised, are then drenched in a lush date molasses tahini drizzle. Topped with crispy fried onions or shallots and a good handful of coriander, this dish is sweet, savoury and crunchy in all the right places. Serve as a side or as a veggie main.

**SERVES 4 AS A SIDE OR 2 AS A MAIN**
**PREP TIME: 15 MINS**
**COOK TIME: 1 HOUR**

## INGREDIENTS

- 4 medium sweet potatoes, skin on, scrubbed clean
- 2 tbsp olive oil, plus extra for drizzling
- 1 tsp ground cumin
- Handful of chopped fresh coriander
- Drizzle of date molasses
- Sea salt and black pepper

FOR THE DATE MOLASSES TAHINI
- 4 tbsp raw tahini
- 1 tbsp date molasses
- Juice of ½ lemon
- 2 tbsp water

FOR THE CRISPY ONIONS
- Neutral oil (such as avocado, pomace or sunflower oil)
- 1 onion or 3 shallots, very thinly sliced
- 1 tbsp flour or cornflour, for dusting (optional)

## METHOD

**1.** Preheat the oven to 200°C fan (220°C/425°F) and line a baking tray with baking parchment. Prick each sweet potato a couple of times with a fork, then rub them with the olive oil, cumin, salt and pepper. Roast for 35–40 minutes, or until tender all the way through and blistering on the outside.

**2.** While the sweet potatoes roast, make your date molasses tahini. In a small bowl, whisk together the tahini, date molasses, lemon juice, a pinch of sea salt and the water until smooth and pourable. There will be a point where it looks like it's all gone wrong, curdled, seized up and split – ignore it. Push through, keep stirring, and slowly add a touch more water if needed. It'll come back to life and turn silky smooth, promise. Set aside.

**3.** Now for the crispy onions. Heat a shallow layer of oil in a frying pan over a medium heat. Toss the thinly sliced onions or shallots in a little flour or cornflour and shake off the excess. This isn't essential but it will help crisp up the onions. Fry in batches until golden brown and crisp, then drain on kitchen paper and sprinkle with salt.

**4.** Once the sweet potatoes are roasted, take them out of the oven and, using the base of a mug or bowl, gently smash each one to flatten and expose more surface area. Drizzle with a little more olive oil and roast again for 10–15 minutes until the edges are crisp and golden.

**5.** Transfer to a serving platter. Drizzle generously with the date molasses tahini, scatter the crispy onions over the top and finish with coriander and a final flick of date molasses.

DATE MOLASSES

# Sticky Chicken Thighs + Chunky Herb Slaw

GF (use gluten-free soy sauce)

This is the kind of traybake that practically cooks itself and makes the house smell like someone who knows what they're doing lives there. The garlic, ginger and soy give you that deep savoury base, while the date molasses adds glossy, sticky sweetness. It's a proper family crowd-pleaser. Best served with bowls of brown rice and a big, crunchy slaw.

**SERVES 4**
**PREP TIME: 25 MINS (PLUS MARINATING)**
**COOK TIME: 35–40 MINS**

### INGREDIENTS
- 4 garlic cloves, finely grated
- Thumb-sized (about 15g) piece of fresh ginger, peeled and grated
- 3 tbsp date molasses
- 3 tbsp soy sauce
- 1 tbsp rice vinegar or apple cider vinegar
- 1 tbsp toasted sesame oil (or neutral oil)
- 8 boneless, skinless chicken thighs
- 1 tbsp olive oil
- Sea salt and black pepper

FOR THE SLAW
- 2 heaped tbsp Greek yoghurt or Labneh (page 40)
- 1 tbsp mayonnaise (optional)
- 1 tbsp apple cider vinegar or white wine vinegar
- 1 tbsp lemon juice
- 1 tsp date molasses
- ¼ white cabbage (150g), thickly sliced
- ¼ red cabbage (150g), thickly sliced
- 1 large carrot, peeled and julienned (or cut into matchsticks)
- 1 green apple, sliced into thin batons
- 3 spring onions, thinly sliced
- Small bunch each of fresh coriander, fresh mint and flat-leaf parsley, leaves picked and roughly chopped

TO FINISH
- A few spring onions, thinly sliced
- 1 tbsp sesame seeds (optional)
- Handful of fresh coriander, chopped (optional)

### METHOD

**1.** Preheat the oven to 200°C fan (220°C/425°F). Line a baking tray with baking parchment or foil.

**2.** In a large bowl, mix together the garlic, ginger, date molasses, soy sauce, vinegar, sesame oil and a little black pepper. Add the chicken thighs and toss to coat thoroughly. Let it sit for 10 minutes if you've got time, or longer in the fridge. Arrange the chicken thighs on the tray, skin-side up, and drizzle over any extra marinade. Roast for 35–40 minutes, basting halfway through with the pan juices, until the skin is crisp and the sauce has caramelised.

**3.** While the chicken is in the oven, prepare the slaw. Whisk together the yoghurt, mayo (if using, or add another tablespoon of yoghurt), vinegar, lemon juice and date molasses in a bowl. Season with salt and pepper to taste; it should be sharp but creamy and not too sweet.

**4.** Toss the sliced cabbage, carrot, apple, spring onions and herbs in a big bowl. Pour over the dressing and mix well. Hands work best here; you want to massage it slightly to help soften the cabbage a little but still keep the crunch. Let it sit for 5–10 minutes before serving so everything soaks up the dressing a bit.

**5.** Let the chicken rest for a couple of minutes before serving. Scatter with sliced spring onions and sesame seeds and fresh coriander, if you like. Serve with the chunky slaw for crunch and contrast.

# Grilled Peaches, Mozzarella, Date Molasses + Basil

V / GF

I still remember the moment Nitai handed me a forkful of mozzarella and grilled peach, standing in a hot, windowless test kitchen in Brooklyn. One bite and I was no longer there. I was in Tuscany. Or maybe Provence. Or at least somewhere sun-soaked and glorious. It was sweet, fresh, creamy and so stupidly good I nearly cried.

That moment stuck with us and inspired Nitai to write this recipe. It's got all the same magic: sweet, warm peaches straight off the grill; cool creamy mozzarella; a sticky drizzle of date molasses and loads of basil. Basically, summer on a plate. This one's made for long lunches, sticky fingers and not a lot of talking.

**SERVES 2–4**
**PREP TIME: 10 MINS**
**COOK TIME: 5 MINS**

## INGREDIENTS

- 3–4 ripe peaches, halved and stones removed
- Extra virgin olive oil, for brushing and drizzling
- 200g fresh mozzarella, torn into chunks
- 30g date molasses (or more if you're heavy-handed like us)
- Handful of fresh basil leaves, some torn, some left whole
- Sea salt and black pepper
- Small handful of toasted pistachios, crushed (optional)

## METHOD

**1.** Get your grill pan or barbecue searing hot – and we mean really hot. Brush the cut sides of the peaches with olive oil, then whack them flesh-side down on to the grill. Give them 2–3 minutes, just until the flesh gets charred and caramelised but still holds its shape. Take the peaches off the heat and let them cool slightly. You want them warm, not piping.

**2.** Arrange the peaches on a big platter with the torn mozzarella nestled around them. Drizzle generously with date molasses; don't be shy. Follow with a good glug of extra virgin olive oil, scatter over the basil, season with salt and pepper and top with crushed pistachios – these are optional but we highly recommend them for crunch.

**3.** Serve immediately while the peaches are still warm and the mozz is cool. Perfect with grilled bread or just forks, straight from the platter.

DATE MOLASSES

# Lamb Meatballs + Cavolo Nero + Goat's Yoghurt

GF

This one's proper comfort food. Sticky, meaty lamb balls spiced with cumin and coriander, seared until golden, then piled on top of lemony goat's yoghurt and crispy cavolo nero. A drizzle of date molasses at the end takes it into knockout territory.

**SERVES 4–6**
**PREP TIME: 20 MINS**
**COOK TIME: 20 MINS**

## INGREDIENTS

FOR THE MEATBALLS
- 500g lamb mince
- 2 garlic cloves, crushed
- 1 tsp ground cumin
- 1 tsp ground coriander
- 10g flat-leaf parsley, finely chopped
- 1 tbsp date molasses
- Sea salt and black pepper
- Olive oil, for frying

FOR THE CAVOLO NERO
- 1 tbsp olive oil (optional)
- 200g cavolo nero, stalks removed, leaves roughly torn
- 1 tsp sumac

FOR THE GOAT'S YOGHURT BASE
- 200g goat's yoghurt
- 1 tbsp olive oil
- Juice of ½ lemon
- 1 garlic clove, finely grated

TO FINISH
- 2 tbsp chopped pistachios
- Handful of coriander leaves
- Sumac Onions (page 56)
- Drizzle of date molasses
- Sliced okra (optional)

## METHOD

**1.** To make the meatballs, mix all the ingredients except the oil in a bowl and season with salt and pepper. Roll into small balls (about 20g each) – you should get about 24. Heat a splash of olive oil in a frying pan over a medium-high heat and cook the meatballs in batches until browned and cooked through. Set aside.

**2.** Place the same pan back over a medium heat. There's no need to clean it as the lamb fat will give great flavour, but if there is a lot of fat, drain some away so you have 1–2 tablespoons of oil in the pan. Or add a little more olive oil. Throw in the cavolo nero and cook for 2–3 minutes until just wilted and a bit crispy at the edges. Season with the sumac and sea salt.

**3.** In a small bowl, stir together the goat's yoghurt, olive oil, lemon juice and garlic and season with salt.

**4.** To serve, spoon the yoghurt on to a platter. Top with the cavolo nero, then the lamb balls. Scatter with chopped pistachios, coriander leaves, a pile of sumac onions, a generous drizzle of date molasses and the okra (if using).

DATE MOLASSES

# Banana + Date Loaf Cake

Ve / DF (use plant-based yoghurt)

We get it – banana bread had its moment. But this one's different. It's sticky with date molasses, spiced just right, and smugly wholesome thanks to spelt flour and olive oil. It's soft, rich, not too sweet, and the kind of cake you'll pretend is breakfast. Works warm, cold, or straight from the tin.

**MAKES 1 LOAF (SERVES 8–10)**
**PREP TIME: 10 MINS (PLUS COOLING)**
**COOK TIME: 45 MINS**

## INGREDIENTS

- 200g ripe bananas, peeled
- 90g soft dark brown sugar
- 90g date molasses
- 120ml olive oil
- 60ml freshly squeezed orange juice
- 60g yoghurt (dairy or plant-based)
- 1 tsp vanilla paste or extract
- 180g spelt flour (or plain flour if that's what you've got), plus extra for dusting
- 1 tsp baking powder
- 1 tsp bicarbonate of soda
- 1 tsp ground cinnamon
- ¼ tsp ground cardamom (optional, but lovely)
- ¼ tsp salt
- 100g Medjool dates, pitted and roughly chopped
- Small handful of pecans (optional)

## METHOD

**1.** Preheat the oven to 170°C fan (190°C/375°F) and line a 900g loaf tin with baking parchment.

**2.** Blend the bananas, brown sugar, date molasses, olive oil, orange juice, yoghurt and vanilla until smooth and silky – a hand-held stick blender or food processor works a treat.

**3.** In a large bowl, mix the flour, baking powder, bicarb, cinnamon, cardamom (if using) and salt. Pour the wet banana mix into the dry and fold gently until just combined. Don't overmix – you're after tender cake, not rubber. Toss the chopped dates in a little flour, then shake off the excess through a sieve. Fold two-thirds of the dates through the batter and reserve the rest to scatter on top.

**4.** Pour the batter into your lined tin, scatter over the remaining dates and pecans (if using) and bake for 45 minutes, or until a knife poked into the middle comes out clean.

**5.** Turn off the oven, crack the door open and leave the cake inside for 10 minutes. Then remove from the oven and cool completely before slicing – if you can wait that long.

### Tip

Swap the dates for dark chocolate chunks, chopped walnuts, pecans, or whatever's lurking in your cupboard.

DATE MOLASSES

# Yeast Extract

*we love it*

---

We all know what we're talking about here. And we love it. We definitely don't hate it. In fact, I'm fully obsessed. My ultimate guilty pleasure? A piece (or several) of matzo (or really any cracker) slathered with a thick layer of cold salted butter, then a generous swipe of yeast extract (preferably Marmite). I eat it at least three times a week, ideally in bed, with an episode of *Below Deck* or *Real Housewives of Beverly Hills* playing in the background. Honestly, how great does that sound? To Jonathan? Absolutely awful. Me crunching away in bed next to him, watching trashy reality TV, is not exactly the stuff of romance.

But yeast extract isn't just for snacking in bed. It's one of the greatest flavour boosters in the pantry. It's salty, rich and full of umami, and it gives a dish that elusive savoury depth, like you've been slowly cooking something for hours, when actually you just added a spoonful of this black gold. We stir it into aioli; we whisk it into salad dressings; we melt it into marinades. We sneak it into toasted sandwiches and butter glazes. It's our secret weapon when something needs a little *oomph*.

And look, I know yeast extract has a reputation. You either love it or you hate it, right? Wrong. You only think you hate it because you haven't had it *properly*. When it's used with a bit of thought it's transformative. It's the ingredient you didn't know you needed. And by the end of this chapter, you'll be a convert. Or at the very least, you'll stop pretending you hate it.

# Yeast Extract Baharat Chicken Wings
DF

These wings are rich, spicy, sticky and absolutely addictive. The yeast extract brings the umami punch, baharat adds depth and warmth, and sriracha keeps things interesting. Finish with sesame and herbs and you've got the kind of crowd-pleaser you'll keep making on repeat. Eat with your hands and lick those fingers. No shame.

**SERVES 4**
**PREP TIME: 15 MINS (PLUS MARINATING)**
**COOK TIME: 35–40 MINS**

### INGREDIENTS
- 2 tbsp yeast extract (we use Marmite)
- 4 tbsp soy sauce
- 2 tbsp sriracha
- 2 tbsp sweet paprika
- 1 tbsp olive oil
- 3 tbsp honey
- 2 tsp baharat spice blend
- 1kg chicken wings, separated into flats and drumettes
- Sea salt and black pepper

TO SERVE
- Sesame seeds
- Handful of chopped flat-leaf parsley or coriander
- Yeast Extract Aioli (page 120)

### METHOD

**1.** Preheat the oven to 200°C fan (220°C/425°F) and line a baking tray with baking parchment or foil.

**2.** In a large bowl, whisk together the yeast extract, soy sauce, sriracha, sweet paprika, olive oil, honey, baharat and some salt and pepper until smooth and glossy. Chuck in the wings and toss to coat, make sure every bit's covered in that magic. If you've got time, let them marinate for at least an hour (or even overnight in the fridge) to really soak up the flavour.

**3.** Lay the wings out in a single layer on the lined tray, making sure they're not crowded. Roast for 35-40 minutes, flipping halfway, until the skins are caramelised and crisp. If you want them extra charred, pop them under a hot grill for the final 2-3 minutes.

**4.** Finish with a shower of sesame seeds and a handful of chopped parsley or coriander. Serve hot, preferably with a big bowl of yeast extract aioli for dipping and something fresh and crunchy on the side.

# Grilled Cheese Toastie + Onion Marmalade + Yeast Extract Butter

V

Crispy, melty, salty-sweet and just a little bit outrageous, in the best way. This toastie is one of those things you make once and then wonder why you ever bothered with plain cheese on toast. The onion marmalade is sticky and rich, the yeast extract butter brings that umami hit, and the whole thing grills into a golden, bubbling masterpiece. Pair it with pickles and a side of Harissa Fennel Salad (page 42).

**SERVES 2**
**PREP TIME: 15 MINS**
**COOK TIME: 45 MINS**

### INGREDIENTS
- 2 slices of your favourite good bread
- 70g melting cheese (Cheddar, Gruyère, or whatever's in the fridge), grated or sliced

FOR THE ONION MARMALADE
(MAKES 1 250ML JAR)
- 2 tbsp olive oil
- 3 large red onions, thinly sliced
- 2 tbsp brown sugar
- 2 tbsp balsamic vinegar
- 1 tbsp red wine vinegar
- Sea salt and black pepper

FOR THE YEAST EXTRACT BUTTER
(MAKES 280G)
- 250g butter, softened
- 30g yeast extract (we use Marmite)

### METHOD

**1.** Start with the onion marmalade. Heat the olive oil in a pan over a low heat, then add the sliced onions and a pinch of salt. Cook slowly for 20–30 minutes, stirring occasionally, until soft and caramelised. Add the brown sugar, balsamic vinegar and red wine vinegar, then let everything bubble and thicken for another 10 minutes until sticky and jammy. Taste, adjust the seasoning, then let it cool before storing in a jar. It will keep for weeks in the fridge and you can use it on everything – toasties, burgers, cheese boards, or just a spoon straight to the mouth.

**2.** While that's going, mash together the softened butter and yeast extract in a bowl until smooth. You'll only need a bit for this recipe but trust us – make the full batch. It keeps well in the fridge and is absolute gold on toast, veg, eggs or a roast chicken.

**3.** Take your bread and spread yeast extract butter on one side of each slice. On the other side of one slice, slather on a good layer of the onion marmalade. Top with a generous handful of grated or sliced cheese. Close the sandwich with the other slice, buttered side out.

**4.** Heat a frying pan over a medium heat. Place the sandwich in the pan and grill for 2–3 minutes on each side, pressing it down lightly so everything fuses together into golden, cheesy perfection. The outside should be crisp and deeply bronzed, the inside a bubbling mess of molten joy.

**5.** Cut it in half and serve immediately. Pickles on the side are non-negotiable, cutting through the richness and keeping you going back in for more.

FACING PAGE
Also shown: Harissa Fennel Salad (page 42)

YEAST EXTRACT

# Slow-cooked Lamb Shanks + Yeast Extract Butter Potatoes

This is proper comfort food. Rich, tender lamb that falls off the bone, swimming in a dark, sticky baharat and date molasses sauce, with yeast extract butter potatoes that are salty, glossy, and completely addictive. The kind of dish that makes you want to cancel plans and stay in with a bottle of red.

**SERVES 4**
**PREP TIME: 30 MINS**
**COOK TIME: 2½–3 HOURS**

### INGREDIENTS
- 4 lamb shanks (about 300g each)
- 3-4 tbsp olive oil
- 1 onion, quartered
- 2 carrots, cut into big chunks
- 3 celery sticks, chopped into big chunks
- 1 leek, chopped into big chunks
- 1 whole garlic bulb, halved horizontally
- 1 litre chicken or vegetable stock
- 100g date molasses
- 2 tbsp baharat spice blend
- A few sprigs of thyme
- Sea salt and black pepper
- Small handful of chopped flat-leaf parsley, to garnish

FOR THE YEAST EXTRACT BUTTER POTATOES
- 800g new potatoes, halved or quartered if large
- 45g butter
- 1-2 tbsp yeast extract (we use Marmite) (to taste)
- Small handful of finely chopped chives, to garnish

### METHOD

**1.** Preheat the oven to 170°C fan (190°C/375°F). Season the lamb shanks all over with salt and pepper, then heat the olive oil in a large cast-iron casserole or deep roasting tray over a medium-high heat and sear the lamb on all sides until properly browned. Take your time; it's all about building flavour. Once browned, remove the lamb and set aside.

**2.** Add the quartered onion to the same casserole or roasting tray and stir well, scraping up all those caramelised bits from the bottom. Add the carrots, celery, leek and garlic and cook for about 5-10 minutes until they start to soften. Return the lamb shanks to the pan, pour in the stock, date molasses and baharat and chuck in a few sprigs of thyme. Cover tightly with a lid or foil and pop it in the oven for 2½ hours. You're looking for meat that falls off the bone and a sauce that's dark and glossy.

**3.** While the lamb's doing its thing, get on with the potatoes. Boil the potatoes in salted water for 15-20 minutes until fork-tender. Melt the butter in a small pan, stir in the yeast extract and whisk until smooth; it will emulsify after a minute or two. Drain the potatoes and toss them straight back into the pot. Pour over the yeast extract butter and toss until every spud is glistening. Season with a touch of salt and pepper and keep warm until ready to serve.

**4.** When the lamb is done, remove it gently from the pan and set aside. Strain the sauce into a clean pan, skim any excess fat from the top and simmer the sauce until it's reduced by half. Taste and adjust the seasoning. Plate up with a big spoonful of yeast extract potatoes with a scattering of chives, a lamb shank, and lashings of sticky, rich sauce. Sprinkle over some parsley.

YEAST EXTRACT

# Roasted Cabbage, Yeast Extract Aioli + Pickled Kale

We're a bit obsessed with hispi cabbage at Farmer J. It's one of those humble ingredients that's criminally underrated, until you roast it. Then it turns sweet, nutty and golden-edged with buttery-soft leaves that hold their shape like a dream. We love it so much we've made it the star of this dish. Add a few Parmesan shavings and you've got a dish that's earthy, salty, tangy and full of crunch. Serve it as a starter, veggie main or just a banging side. It's that good.

**SERVES 4 AS A SIDE OR 2 AS A MAIN**
**PREP TIME: 30 MINUTES (PLUS PICKLING)**
**COOK TIME: 50 MINS–1 HOUR**

### INGREDIENTS

- 1 large hispi or white cabbage, cut into 6-8 chunky wedges (core intact)
- Olive oil for drizzling
- 50g roasted cashews, crushed or left whole
- 30g Parmesan shavings
- 50g Quick Pickled Red Onion (optional; page 161)
- Sea salt and black pepper

**FOR THE PICKLED KALE**

- 100g kale, tough stems removed
- 100ml apple cider vinegar
- 50ml water
- 1 tbsp caster sugar
- 1 tsp sea salt

**FOR THE YEAST EXTRACT AIOLI**

- 1 free-range egg yolk
- 1 tsp Dijon mustard
- 1 garlic clove, grated
- 150ml neutral oil (such as avocado oil)
- Squeeze of lemon
- Pinch of salt
- 1–1½ tsp Marmite (to taste)

### METHOD

**1.** First, make the aioli. Whisk the egg yolk, mustard and garlic, then slowly drizzle in the oil while whisking continuously until thick. Finish with a squeeze of lemon and a pinch of salt, then stir in your yeast extract.

**2.** Preheat the oven to 160°C fan (180°C/350°F) and line a baking tray with baking parchment. Place the cabbage wedges on the lined tray, drizzle with olive oil and season with salt and a very generous grind of black pepper. Roast for 45-50 minutes, flipping once, until the edges are golden and the centres are buttery soft.

**3.** While that's going, make your pickled kale. Put the kale in a bowl. Combine the vinegar, water, sugar and salt in a pan, bring to a simmer, then pour over the kale. Let it pickle for 20-30 minutes, then drain and pat dry.

**4.** Make the aioli and stir in the yeast extract until evenly combined.

**5.** Time to plate. Arrange the roasted cabbage on a big serving platter. Tuck the pickled kale around the wedges and spoon over the yeast extract aioli – it should tumble and melt into the nooks. Scatter over the roasted cashews and add your Parmesan shavings. If you're going all in, finish with a few slices of pickled red onion for a punchy hit of acid.

YEAST EXTRACT

# NUTS, Seeds & CRUNCHES

| **Pitta Chips** *124* | **Walnuts** *132* | **Dukkah** *140* | **Sesame Seeds** *150* |

# Pitta Chips

*a welcome crunch*

---

Trays of leftover pitta, brushed with olive oil, then sprinkled with salt and za'atar and roasted until golden – what's not to like? They're not here to steal the show, just to make everything else better. Add a handful to a salad or dip and suddenly you've got texture, contrast and that irresistible moreish bite.

We love them smashed into fattoush, scooped through hummus, or scattered over something soft and creamy – labneh, tzatziki, aubergine – anything that needs a little lift. They add crunch, sure, but they also soak up dressings and hold on to spices in a way that makes everything taste more put together.

You can make them (see our easy recipe) or buy them in if you're short on time. Once you've had them fresh out of the oven, still warm and crisp, it'll be hard to go back, but no judgement either way. Just make sure they're good and salty and you've got plenty of them.

# Pitta Chips

Ve / DF

Crispy, salty, herby and totally snackable. These pitta chips are dangerously easy to make and even easier to eat. Perfect on their own, with dips, or crunched over a salad. Just check your pittas are dairy-free (if that's important to you); some supermarket ones sneak milk in.

**SERVES 4 AS A SNACK OR TOPPER**
**PREP TIME: LESS THAN 5 MINS**
**COOK TIME: 10 MINS**

### INGREDIENTS
- 5–6 pitta breads (check they're dairy-free)
- 4–5 tbsp olive oil
- 2 tbsp sumac
- 3 tbsp za'atar
- 1 tsp of sea salt

### METHOD

**1.** Preheat the oven to 200°C fan (220°C/425°F).

**2.** Cut the pittas into wedges, big triangles or small chips – whatever takes your fancy – and place in a large bowl. Give them a decent drizzle of olive oil and toss them around so they're all coated. Sprinkle over the sumac, za'atar and a good pinch of sea salt – don't be shy here.

**3.** Lay them out on a baking tray in a single layer and bake for 8–10 minutes until golden and crisp. Shake them after 4–5 minutes and keep an eye on them near the end as they go from golden to burnt pretty quickly. Let them cool slightly, then serve. Store any extras in an airtight container for up to 1 week.

# Kale Caesar

This one's a twist on the classic. We've swapped out the croutons for golden shards of crisp pitta chips, used a base of hearty greens like kale and cavolo nero, and thrown in a bit of feta for that salty edge. The Caesar dressing is sharp, creamy and clings to the leaves just right. If you've got good greens, this salad will never feel like the side act.

**SERVES 3–4 AS A MAIN OR 4–6 AS A SIDE**
**PREP TIME: 15 MINS**

### INGREDIENTS
- 100g kale, tough stems discarded and leaves torn
- 50g cavolo nero, tough stems discarded and leaves torn
- 150g lettuce (iceberg, cos, baby gem), torn
- 50g Quick Pickled Red Onion (page 161), plus 1 tbsp pickling liquid
- Pinch of sea salt
- 100g broccoli florets, roughly chopped
- 50–70g Pitta Chips (page 125)
- 1 ripe avocado, sliced
- 50g crumbled feta, for topping

### FOR THE CAESAR DRESSING
- 1 tbsp olive oil
- 1 tsp avocado or pomace oil (or just use more olive oil)
- Juice of ½ lemon
- 1 heaped tsp grated Parmesan
- 2 heaped tsp mayonnaise
- 1 tsp Dijon mustard
- ½ small garlic clove, finely grated
- Sea salt and black pepper

### METHOD

**1.** Chuck the kale, cavolo nero and lettuce pieces into a large bowl. Add the tablespoon of pickle juice from the onions and the salt and scrunch the leaves until they soften slightly. Add the broccoli and the pickled onion. Break your pitta chips into shards (if large) and scatter them across the salad.

**2.** Now for the dressing. Whisk together all the ingredients until you have a dressing that's silky and smooth. Drizzle over the salad but don't drown it – you want to coat not soak – and toss gently until the greens are evenly dressed.

**3.** Top with sliced avocado and a solid handful of feta crumbs. Serve immediately while the chips still snap. Extra pitta chips on the side never hurt.

PITTA CHIPS

# Dips + Chips

These dips are built for sharing. Whether you're piling them on to warm bread or loading up a pitta chip, they bring layers of flavour, richness, heat, crunch and tang. These dips are made for passing around a table with mates, drinks, and something crisp and salty to scoop it all up. If you only ever make one thing to go with your pitta chips, make it one of these. Or better yet, make all three.

## Roasted Aubergine + Tahini Yoghurt + Brown Butter
V

The holy trinity: smoky aubergine, creamy tahini and nutty brown butter. If you've never spooned brown butter over a cold dip before, welcome to your new obsession. The crunch comes from dukkah or pistachios and the whole thing is outrageously moreish.

**SERVES 4–6 AS A SIDE**
**PREP TIME: 50 MINS (PLUS SALTING)**
**COOK TIME: 45 MINS–1 HOUR**

### INGREDIENTS
- 3 large aubergines
- 200g tahini
- 200g full-fat Greek yoghurt
- Zest and juice of 1 lemon
- 1 garlic clove, grated
- Pinch of ground cumin
- 75g unsalted butter (or use salted and skip the end sprinkle)
- Sea salt and white pepper
- About 175ml ice-cold water

### TO SERVE
- 50g crushed roasted pistachios or Classic Dukkah (page 141)
- Extra virgin olive oil
- Fresh herbs – parsley, coriander or dill all work well
- Pitta Chips (page 125)

### METHOD

**1.** Roast the aubergines whole over an open flame (using kitchen tongs to hold them over the flame) or in an oven preheated to 200°C fan (220°C/425°F) until blackened and collapsed. This will take at least an hour in the oven, or 15–20 minutes over a flame. Let them cool, then peel off the skins, sprinkle the flesh with salt and leave in a colander for 30 minutes.

**2.** Mix the tahini, yoghurt, lemon zest and juice, garlic and cumin together until combined and season with salt and white and pepper. Don't worry if your mixture seizes; it will loosen when you add the water. Slowly add the ice-cold water, whisking until creamy and thick. Set aside.

**3.** Melt the butter in a small pan over a low heat and cook gently until it browns and smells nutty. Keep warm.

**4.** Spread the tahini-yoghurt over the base of a platter and roughly tear or chop the aubergine over the top. Drizzle with warm brown butter and finish with the pistachios or dukkah. Drizzle with extra virgin olive oil and sprinkle over the herbs and a pinch of flaky sea salt. Serve with pitta chips.

PITTA CHIPS

**Tip**

Make the lamb and sauce a day ahead, then reheat gently before serving. The pitta chips can be made a few days ahead – just make sure you store in an airtight container.

# Walnuts

*texture and richness*

---

Walnuts. We love them. Toasted, caramelised, blitzed into a sauce, or crumbled over roasted veg, they're one of those ingredients that quietly show up again and again at Farmer J. They bring texture, richness, and just the right hit of bitterness to balance out sweetness and salt. Plus, they've got that earthy flavour that makes a salad or slaw feel more like a proper meal.

They're excellent friends to za'atar, yoghurt, honey, date molasses, tahini . . . the pantry staples we already adore. Whether it's a crunchy topping on a soft aubergine or a nutty backbone to a punchy dressing, walnuts hold their own without showing off.

Sweet or savoury, they belong. So this section is our ode to walnuts, an underrated member of the pantry.

# Date Molasses + Za'atar Caramelised Walnuts

Ve / GF / DF

The salty-sweet snack you didn't know you needed. These walnuts get glossy and golden in the oven, with the sharp tang of za'atar and that deep, almost burnt-sugar stickiness from date molasses. We scatter them in salads, over roasted veg, or just eat them by the fistful straight off the tray.

**MAKES ABOUT 200G**
**PREP TIME: 5 MINS (PLUS COOLING)**
**COOK TIME: 5-7 MINS**

## INGREDIENTS
- 200g walnuts
- 30g date molasses
- 2 tbsp za'atar
- Generous pinch of sea salt

## METHOD

**1.** Preheat the oven to 160°C fan (180°C/350°F) and line a baking tray with baking parchment.

**2.** In a mixing bowl, toss the walnuts with the date molasses, za'atar and sea salt until every crevice of every nut is coated – sticky is what we're after. Spread the walnuts out on the lined tray, making sure they're in a single layer.

**3.** Bake for 5-7 minutes, giving them a stir halfway through so they caramelise evenly. Keep an eye on them: nuts go from golden to burnt in a flash. Take them out when they're toasty and smelling incredible. Let them cool on the tray; they'll firm up as they cool.

**WALNUTS**

### Tip
Add a pinch of chilli flakes or smoked paprika if you want a bit of a kick.

# Castelfranco Salad + Honey Walnut Dressing

V / GF / DF

This one's got everything going for it: bitter leaves, creamy avocado, a sweet-sour punch from the dressing, and a hit of crunch from those caramelised walnuts (yes, the ones you now keep in a jar like snacks). It's a real showpiece salad, built to cut through a roast or hold its own at any table. Big flavours, no fuss.

**SERVES 4–6**
**PREP TIME: 15 MINS**

### INGREDIENTS
- 2 small heads of Belgian (white) endive, torn by hand
- 1 small head of red endive
- ½ small head of cos lettuce
- 3–4 small radishes, thinly sliced
- 1 ripe avocado, sliced
- Small handful of Date Molasses & Za'atar Caramelised Walnuts (page 133)
- Small handful of dill, chopped

FOR THE WALNUT DRESSING
- 1 tsp grated garlic
- 100g walnuts
- 1½ tbsp Dijon mustard
- 2 tbsp chopped fresh dill
- 2½ tbsp honey
- 5 tbsp red wine vinegar
- 100ml almond milk
- 175ml neutral oil (such as avocado, pomace or sunflower oil)
- Generous pinch of sea salt

### METHOD
**1.** For the dressing, throw the garlic, half the walnuts, mustard, dill, honey, red wine vinegar, almond milk, oil and salt into a blender. Blitz until smooth and creamy. Lightly crush the remaining walnuts and add to the blender. Pulse just once or twice, you want bits, not mush. Set aside.

**2.** In a big bowl, mix the white and red endive, cos and radishes. Season with a pinch of salt. Drizzle over the walnut dressing; you want everything nicely coated but not swimming.

**3.** Plate up the salad, scatter with sliced avocado, caramelised walnuts and a final hit of chopped dill.

# Kohlrabi Carpaccio + Sesame + Parmesan
GF

Paper-thin slices of crisp kohlrabi are elevated to something truly special with a bright citrus dressing, nutty sesame, and creamy Parmesan. This dish is a testament to how the simplest ingredients can create something spectacular, light, elegant, full of flavour and so easy to make.

**SERVES 2–4 AS A STARTER OR LIGHT SIDE**
**PREP TIME: 15 MINS**

## INGREDIENTS
- 1 medium kohlrabi, peeled
- Juice of 1 lemon
- 1 tbsp olive oil
- 1 tsp toasted sesame oil
- Generous pinch of sea salt
- 2 tbsp sesame seeds (mix of black and white)
- 30g Parmesan, shaved or grated
- 1 tbsp finely chopped chives
- Generous handful of walnuts, lightly toasted
- 5-7 drops of truffle oil (optional)

**METHOD**

**1.** First, slice the kohlrabi. Using a sharp knife or mandoline, slice the kohlrabi as thinly as possible – it should be almost translucent. Arrange the kohlrabi slices in a fan or overlapping pattern on a flat serving plate.

**2.** To make the dressing, whisk together the lemon juice, olive oil, sesame oil and sea salt in a small bowl. (The sesame oil adds a subtle depth that complements the nuttiness of the sesame seeds and Parmesan.) Drizzle the dressing evenly over the kohlrabi slices.

**3.** Sprinkle the sesame seeds over the kohlrabi, followed by the Parmesan and chives. Finish with the toasted walnuts and – if you want an optional flair – 5-7 drops of truffle oil (less is more here).

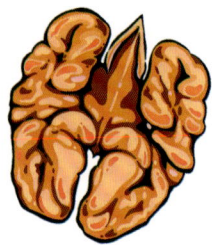

WALNUTS

# Roasted Beetroot, Freekeh + Walnut Salad

V / DF

Here, three ingredients that we can't get enough of come together in a salad that's hearty, earthy and totally satisfying. Roasted beets meet nutty freekeh, with caramelised walnuts bringing that sweet crunch. But the real game-changer? A creamy beetroot and walnut tahini spread layered underneath like a savoury hummus. Big flavour, brilliant textures and yes, very, very pink.

**SERVES 4**
**PREP TIME: 20 MINS**
**COOK TIME: 40 MINS**

## INGREDIENTS

- 6 small beetroot or 4 medium, scrubbed
- 200g freekeh
- 100g Date Molasses & Za'atar Caramelised Walnuts (page 133)
- 2 tbsp olive oil
- Sea salt and black pepper
- Large handful of chopped fresh parsley, mint or dill

FOR THE DRESSING
- 3 tbsp olive oil
- 1 tbsp lemon juice
- 1 tbsp pomegranate molasses
- 1 tsp Dijon mustard
- 1 tsp ground cumin (optional)

FOR THE BEETROOT
& WALNUT TAHINI SPREAD
- 100g walnuts
- 2 cooked beetroot, peeled and diced (from above)
- 3 tbsp tahini
- 2 tbsp olive oil
- 1 tbsp lemon juice
- 1 garlic clove, grated

## METHOD

**1.** Preheat the oven to 200°C fan (220°C/425°F). Place the whole, scrubbed beetroot in a roasting dish, drizzle with a little olive oil, and cover tightly with foil. Roast for 40-50 minutes, until tender when pierced with a knife. Let them cool slightly, then peel and dice. Set aside 2 beetroot for the spread, and the rest for the salad.

**2.** Start with the spread. Put all the ingredients into a food processor and blend until smooth and thick, adding 2-3 tablespoons of water a spoonful at a time to loosen and get it silky. Season with salt and pepper and set aside.

**3.** Bring 400ml of water to the boil in a saucepan. Add the freekeh, reduce to a simmer and cook for 20-25 minutes until tender but still with bite. Drain and let it cool slightly.

**4.** To make the dressing, whisk together the olive oil, lemon juice, pomegranate molasses, mustard and cumin (if using) and season to taste with salt and pepper.

**5.** In a bowl, toss the diced beetroot, cooked freekeh and caramelised walnuts together. Drizzle over the dressing and toss again gently. Spread the beetroot and walnut tahini across a serving platter or shallow bowl. Spoon the salad on top and finish with a big handful of chopped herbs.

# Tahini Walnut Cookies

V

These are nutty, sweet and just the right amount of crunchy. The tahini makes them smooth and rich, the walnuts give a toasty depth, and that walnut perched on top? Yum. They're a dream with coffee and dangerously moreish straight off the tray.

**MAKES 20–25 COOKIES**
**PREP TIME: 25 MINS (PLUS 1–2 HOURS CHILLING)**
**COOK TIME: 10–12 MINS**

### INGREDIENTS
- 115g unsalted butter, softened
- 130g caster sugar
- 65g honey
- 100g tahini
- 180g plain flour
- 1 tsp baking powder
- Good pinch of salt
- 25g walnuts, finely chopped
- 25g white sesame seeds (for coating)
- 20–25 walnut halves (½ walnut per cookie)

### METHOD

**1.** In a stand mixer (or using a hand-held electric whisk), beat the butter and sugar on medium speed for about 5 minutes until smooth, pale and fluffy. Add the honey and tahini and keep mixing until it turns silky and caramel-like.

**2.** Sift the flour, baking powder and salt into a separate bowl. Add it bit by bit to the wet mix, beating gently until you've got a soft dough. Fold in the chopped walnuts.

**3.** Divide the dough into two or three logs, each about 4–5cm in diameter. Gently roll each log in sesame seeds until coated, then place on a tray and chill in the fridge or freezer for at least 1–2 hours until firm.

**4.** When you are ready to bake, preheat the oven to 160°C fan (180°C/350°F) and line one or two baking trays with baking parchment.

**5.** Slice the chilled logs into rounds about 2cm thick. Lay them out on the lined trays and press a walnut half into each one.

**6.** Bake for 10–12 minutes, or until golden just around the edges. They'll be crumbly and fragile while hot so let them cool on the tray to firm up.

### Tip
Don't want 25 cookies? Freeze the logs whole, then just slice off what you need and bake straight from frozen (just give them an extra minute or two in the oven).

# Dukkah

*crunchy, nutty and deeply aromatic*

---

Let's talk dukkah. This Middle Eastern spice and nut blend is one of those magical ingredients that makes everything taste better. Traditionally from Egypt, the name comes from the Arabic word for 'to pound' and that's how it's made: nuts, seeds and spices are toasted and bashed together until crumbly; coarse but not powdery. The blend varies depending on who's making it; some go heavy on hazelnuts, others swear by almonds. Add fennel seeds or thyme, use black pepper or sumac – there are no rules. We've even made an Asian-inspired version with nori and sesame. Once you start making your own, you won't stop.

At Farmer J, we use it all the time, sprinkled over roasted veg, salads and labneh. It brings a welcome crunch to soft textures, a toasty depth to creamy dips, and elevates a humble salad. It's also great mixed into breadcrumbs or folded through yoghurt for a bit of body. We've even been known to toss it over fruit with a little date molasses. Don't knock it 'til you've tried it!

You can buy it, sure, but making it yourself means you get to play. Swap in different nuts, dial the spice up or down, toast it darker or keep it light. It keeps well in a jar, so go on, make a batch and keep it in the pantry for those 'something's missing' moments.

# Classic Dukkah

Ve / GF / DF

This is the OG. An Egyptian blend of toasted nuts, seeds and spices that's warm, nutty and ridiculously good on everything. We serve it with olive oil and warm pitta as a dip, but it also transforms roasted veg, grilled chicken and even eggs.

**MAKES ABOUT 250G**
**PREP TIME: 10 MINS**

### INGREDIENTS
- 50g hazelnuts
- 50g whole almonds
- 50g shelled pistachios
- 50g pine nuts
- 30g sesame seeds
- 1 tbsp coriander seeds
- 1 tbsp cumin seeds
- 1 tsp black pepper
- 1 tsp sea salt

### METHOD

**1.** In a dry frying pan, toast the hazelnuts, almonds, pistachios, pine nuts, sesame seeds, coriander and cumin seeds over a medium heat for 3-5 minutes, stirring regularly until golden and fragrant. Let it all cool.

**2.** Pulse everything in a food processor or spice grinder until it's coarse and crumbly but not powdery (you want crunch). Add the black pepper and salt, give it one final pulse and you're done.

**3.** Store in an airtight jar for up to 2 weeks.

# Asian Nori Dukkah

Ve / GF / DF

A punchier twist on the classic. This one's packed with roasted sesame, nori, ginger and black pepper, think Japanese furikake meets Egyptian spice mix. Perfect on rice bowls, noodles, or even a piece of avo' toast.

**MAKES ABOUT 6 TBSP**
**PREP TIME: 5 MINS**

### INGREDIENTS
- 30g sesame seeds
- 1 tbsp coriander seeds
- 10g nori sheets (crushed or torn)
- 1 tbsp ground ginger
- 1 tsp black pepper
- 1 tsp sea salt

### METHOD

**1.** Toast the sesame seeds and coriander seeds in a dry frying pan over a medium heat for 2-3 minutes until fragrant. Let them cool slightly.

**2.** Combine with the nori, ground ginger, black pepper and salt. Pulse in a spice grinder or food processor until you've got a coarse mix. Taste and tweak the salt or ginger if needed.

**3.** Store in an airtight container for up to 1 month.

# Citrus Endive Dukkah Salad

V / GF

Bright, bitter, sweet, creamy, crunchy – it's all happening here. The key is contrast: bitter endive, juicy citrus, creamy aioli dressing and a hit of crunch from our classic dukkah. It's fresh, it's vibrant, and it's perfect with grilled meat, or just a hunk of bread and some labneh on the side.

**SERVES 4–6**
**PREP TIME: 20 MINS**

## INGREDIENTS

- 2 heads of Belgian (white) endive
- 1 small head of red endive
- 2 oranges, peeled and segmented
- 1 grapefruit, peeled and segmented
- ½ pomelo, peeled and segmented (optional, but worth it)
- 60g celeriac, peeled and diced into small cubes
- Quick Pickled Red Onion (page 161)
- 2 tbsp Classic Dukkah, plus extra to finish (page 141)

FOR THE AIOLI
- 1 free-range egg yolk
- 1 tsp Dijon mustard
- 1 garlic clove, grated
- 150ml neutral oil (such as avocado, pomace or sunflower oil)
- Squeeze of lemon juice
- Pinch of salt

FOR THE HONEY & CRÈME FRAÎCHE AIOLI DRESSING
- 2 tbsp honey
- 2 tbsp crème fraîche
- 5 tbsp aioli (see above)
- 1 tbsp Dijon mustard
- 1 tbsp white wine vinegar
- 2 tbsp olive oil
- Sea salt and black pepper

## METHOD

**1.** First, make the aioli. Whisk the egg yolk, mustard and garlic, then slowly drizzle in the oil while whisking continuously until thick. Finish with a squeeze of lemon and a pinch of salt.

**2.** Tear the endive into big rustic pieces and chuck them into a large bowl. Add the citrus segments to the salad, along with the diced celeriac and pickled onion. Sprinkle over the dukkah.

**3.** For the dressing, in a small bowl, whisk together the honey, crème fraîche and aioli until smooth. Add the mustard and vinegar, then slowly drizzle in the olive oil, whisking the whole time so it emulsifies. Season with salt and pepper and taste; it should be tangy, creamy, sweet and sharp all at once. Pour the dressing over the salad just before serving and toss gently to coat. Finish with a sprinkle of dukkah and that's it.

DUKKAH

# Roasted Leeks + Dukkah Crumble

V / GF

This one's all about layering textures. Sweet, tender roasted leeks are topped with a herby chimichurri and a crunchy hit of dukkah, then finished with a dollop of crème fraîche to pull it all together. Simple, bold and full of flavour, serve it warm or at room temperature. Works as a side dish or as a starter.

The chimichurri quantities below make more than you need for this recipe but it will keep well in the fridge for up to a week and is excellent on steak, roasted veg, fish, chicken, or eggs.

**SERVES 3–4**
**PREP TIME: 30 MINS**
**COOK TIME: 25 MINS**

### INGREDIENTS
FOR THE ROASTED LEEKS
- 4 large leeks
- 2 tbsp olive oil
- Sea salt and black pepper
- 2 tbsp crème fraîche, to serve

FOR THE ALMOND DUKKAH
- 50g whole almonds
- 50g shelled pistachios
- 50g pine nuts
- 30g sesame seeds
- 1 tbsp coriander seeds
- 1 tbsp cumin seeds
- 1 tsp sea salt
- 1 tsp black pepper

FOR THE CHIMICHURRI
- 100g red chillies (about 4), deseeded and finely chopped
- 250g parsley, finely chopped
- 250g coriander, finely chopped
- 40g garlic (about 10 cloves), grated
- 50g fresh mint, finely chopped
- 20g fresh oregano, finely chopped
- 75ml white wine vinegar
- 300ml olive oil

### METHOD
**1.** Preheat the oven to 200°C fan (220°C/425°F).

**2.** Trim the leeks but keep the root more or less intact, then split them lengthways. Lay the leeks cut-side up on a baking tray, drizzle with olive oil, season well and roast for 20–25 minutes until golden and soft but still holding their shape.

**3.** While the leeks roast, make the dukkah: spread the almonds, pistachios, pine nuts, sesame seeds, coriander and cumin seeds out on a baking tray. Toast in the oven for 4–5 minutes until golden and fragrant, checking regularly so they don't burn. Let them cool completely, then pulse in a food processor until coarse and crunchy. Stir in the salt and pepper and set aside.

**4.** In a large bowl, mix all the chimichurri ingredients together, then taste and adjust the seasoning. Let it sit for 10–15 minutes to let the flavours come together.

**5.** To serve, slice the roasted leeks into long chunky pieces and layer on to a platter. Spoon over 2–3 tablespoons of chimichurri (or more if you fancy it) and add a generous dollop of crème fraiche. Finish with a heavy scattering of the almond dukkah (store what's left in an airtight container for up to 2 weeks).

DUKKAH

# Green Dukkah Slaw

Ve / GF / DF

This is not a shy salad. With crunchy vegetables, tangy pickled accents, and the irresistible nutty crunch of dukkah, it's a bold, punchy accompaniment to any meal. Whether piled high in a sandwich, served alongside grilled meat or fish, or as the star of a veggie feast, this is a salad with attitude. This slaw can be prepared up to 2 hours in advance and stored in the fridge. The flavours will only deepen and improve, though be sure to give it a quick toss before serving.

**SERVES 2–4**
**PREP TIME: 20 MINS (PLUS PICKLING)**

## INGREDIENTS

- 250g hispi cabbage, shredded
- 1 large head of broccoli, about 300g, stem thinly sliced and florets finely chopped
- 2 tbsp Quick Pickled Red Onion (page 161 or shop-bought), finely chopped
- 1 tbsp chopped pickled green chilli (for a fiery kick)
- 2 tbsp chopped pickled cucumber (see below)
- 3 tbsp Classic Dukkah (page 141)
- 1 tbsp chopped flat-leaf parsley

FOR THE PICKLED CUCUMBER
- 1 cucumber, thinly sliced
- White wine vinegar
- Water
- Pinch of salt
- 1 tsp sugar

FOR THE DRESSING
- 4 tbsp olive oil
- 4 tbsp fresh lemon juice

## METHOD

**1.** First, pickle the cucumber. Add the cucumber to a jar, then cover with equal parts vinegar and water, plus the salt and sugar. Leave to pickle for at least 30 minutes.

**2.** Then prepare the dressing. Add the olive oil, lemon juice and a pinch of sea salt to a jar with a tight-fitting lid. Secure the lid and give it a good shake until it emulsifies into a silky, tangy dressing. (You can also whisk everything together in a small bowl if you're feeling less dramatic, but a jar is best, trust me.)

**3.** Next, assemble the slaw. In a large mixing bowl, toss together the hispi cabbage, broccoli, pickled onion, pickled green chilli, pickled cucumber and 2 tablespoons of the dukkah. Pour over the dressing and mix thoroughly to coat every piece.

**4.** To serve, scatter over the remaining dukkah for crunch and add a sprinkle of fresh parsley for a hit of colour.

# Raw Courgette Salad + Lemon Vinaigrette + Dukkah

V / GF

A no-cook summer salad with crunch, zing and serious freshness. Thin courgette ribbons are tossed with a sharp lime and dill vinaigrette, tangy pickled onion, briny olives and a hefty sprinkle of crunchy dukkah. It's light but punchy and when slathered on a bed of creamy labneh or topped with dollops of fresh ricotta, it becomes a dish that feels far more indulgent than it ought to. Perfect as a side but also holds its own as a light lunch.

**SERVES 4**
**PREP TIME: 15 MINS**

### INGREDIENTS
- 2 green courgettes (see Tip)
- Labneh (page 40) or fresh ricotta
- Handful of fresh mint, leaves picked
- Handful of fresh dill, roughly chopped
- Quick Pickled Red Onion, to taste (page 161)
- Handful of black olives, pitted and chopped
- Handful of Classic Dukkah (page 141)

FOR THE LIME & DILL VINAIGRETTE
- 40ml lime juice
- 60ml olive oil
- Generous pinch of salt
- 2 tsp Dijon mustard
- 1 tsp coriander or dill seeds
- Handful of fresh dill, chopped

### METHOD
**1.** Slice the courgettes thinly into rounds or long ribbons. A mandoline works beautifully if you've got one, otherwise a sharp knife does the trick.

**2.** Make the vinaigrette: whisk together the lime juice, olive oil, salt, mustard, coriander or dill seeds and chopped dill. Taste and adjust as needed; it should be punchy, bright and a little bit grassy.

**3.** If you're using labneh, spread a generous swoosh across the base of your serving plate. Layer the courgette slices over the top, then scatter over the mint, dill, pickled onion and olives. Drizzle with the vinaigrette and finish with a proper handful of dukkah for crunch. If you're using ricotta instead of labneh, just spoon it over the top before serving. Let it sit for 5 minutes if you've got the patience; it helps everything soak up the vinaigrette and mellow slightly.

DUKKAH

**Tip**
Look for Trombetta or Graziani courgette varieties; they are less watery and will give you a better texture.

# Seared Tuna + Asian Nori Dukkah + Rice Noodle Salad

GF (use gluten-free soy sauce) / DF

This dish is a banger – it's clean, light, full of texture and punch. The tuna's quickly seared tataki-style, then crusted with our Asian nori dukkah for that savoury, umami crunch. Underneath is a crisp cabbage and noodle salad dressed with rice vinegar, lime and sesame that is bright, sharp and balanced. You need proper sashimi-grade tuna for this as you're eating it practically raw in the middle. Get the best you can from a fishmonger you trust. It should be deep red, glossy, and smell like absolutely nothing.

**SERVES 3–4**
**PREP TIME: 30 MINS**
**COOK TIME: 5–10 MINS**

## INGREDIENTS

- 3 fresh tuna loins/steaks (about 180–200g each)
- 1 tsp soy sauce (optional)
- 1 tbsp olive oil
- 1 tbsp toasted sesame oil
- 1 tbsp hoisin sauce or mirin
- 100g Asian Nori Dukkah (page 141), plus extra to finish
- Sea salt and black pepper
- Roughly chopped fresh coriander and lime wedges, to serve

FOR THE SALAD
- 100g rice noodles (we like vermicelli but flat noodles also work)
- ½ small white cabbage (about 150g), finely shredded
- 1 carrot, peeled and cut into matchsticks
- 1 cucumber, cut into matchsticks
- 2 spring onions, thinly sliced
- 1 tbsp pickled ginger, finely chopped
- 1 tbsp chopped fresh coriander
- 1 tbsp rice vinegar
- 1 tbsp toasted sesame oil
- 1 tbsp soy sauce
- 1 tsp mirin
- 1 tsp lime juice
- 1 tsp toasted sesame seeds (optional)

## METHOD

**1.** Start by prepping the salad. Cook the rice noodles according to the packet instructions, then drain and rinse under cold water. Set aside.

**2.** Add the shredded cabbage, carrot, cucumber, spring onions, pickled ginger and chopped coriander to a large bowl and mix to combine. Add the cooled noodles and toss together.

**3.** Whisk up the rice vinegar, sesame oil, soy sauce, mirin, lime juice and sesame seeds to make a dressing, then pour it over the noodle salad and toss to coat everything.

**4.** Now for the tuna. Pat your steaks/loins dry with kitchen paper. Season with salt and pepper and a tiny splash of soy, if you like. Heat the olive oil and sesame oil in a frying pan until smoking hot, then add the tuna and sear for 1–2 minutes on each side; you want a crisp edge and a raw centre.

**5.** Brush the seared tuna with hoisin or mirin, then roll in the dukkah to coat, pressing it on gently so it sticks. Let the tuna rest for a couple of minutes, then cut into 1cm thick slices.

**6.** Add a big mound of noodle salad to a serving bowl, lay slices of tuna on top and add a final sprinkle of dukkah, some fresh coriander and lime wedges for squeezing.

# Sesame Seeds

*tiny but mighty*

---

You'll find sesame seeds absolutely everywhere in our kitchen. We chuck them on almost anything that'll hold still long enough; think roasted salmon, sticky noodle bowls, shaved veg salads – even the odd curry when it needs that little extra nutty edge. They're one of those ingredients that feel like an afterthought but end up being the bit you remember. A crunch, a toastiness, a whisper of bitterness that makes everything else taste more complete.

What's brilliant about sesame is how well it plays across the board, from Middle Eastern labneh dips and tahini-based dressings to the zing of Asian-style smashed cucumber or a miso-glazed aubergine. You'll find it in our marinades, sprinkled over roasted leeks, or finishing off a rice bowl. Toast them, leave them raw, use white or black, mix them with za'atar or stir them into a paste. However you go, they bring depth and texture without ever shouting about it.

At Farmer J, we treat sesame as if it's a seasoning, like salt or lemon; it's that essential. It's what makes your veg feel a bit more dressed, your protein a bit more deliberate, and your plate that bit more polished.

# Charred Sesame Broccoli + Maple Lemon Ponzu

Ve / GF / DF

This is broccoli done properly, the kind of side dish that ends up stealing the spotlight. It's charred and nutty with sesame, then hit with a sharp-sweet ponzu dressing while it's still hot so it soaks up every drop. Serve it with rice bowls, grilled salmon, or just eat it straight off the tray. And if you're cooking for kids or softer palates, there's a tip below to keep it tender without losing the flavour. (Shown on page 44)

**SERVES 4 AS A SIDE**
**PREP TIME: 10 MINS**
**COOK TIME: 10–12 MINS**

### INGREDIENTS
- 2 heads of broccoli (about 500–600g), broken into florets
- 100ml olive oil
- 1 tbsp toasted sesame oil
- 1 garlic clove, grated
- 2 tbsp sesame seeds (mix of white and black), plus extra to finish

FOR THE MAPLE LEMON PONZU
- Juice of 1 lemon
- 2½ tbsp soy sauce
- 2 tsp maple syrup
- 1 tbsp mirin
- ½ tsp chilli flakes (optional)

### METHOD

**1.** Preheat the oven to 220°C fan (240°C/465°F). You want serious heat here to get that char. Line a large baking tray with baking parchment.

**2.** Toss the broccoli florets into a large bowl with the olive oil, sesame oil, garlic and the sesame seeds. Make sure everything's properly coated. Spread the broccoli on to the lined tray in a single layer; don't overcrowd or it'll steam instead of roast. Roast for 10–12 minutes until the edges are crisp and browned but the stems still have a bit of bite.

**3.** While that's happening, whisk together the lemon juice, soy sauce, maple syrup, mirin and chilli flakes (if using). That's your sharp-sweet-salty hit.

**4.** As soon as the broccoli comes out of the oven, pour over 3 tablespoons of the maple lemon ponzu and toss gently to coat. It should hiss a bit and soak it all up. Finish with a final sprinkle of sesame seeds and serve straight away while it's still warm and crunchy.

### Tip
If you're feeding little mouths or prefer a softer bite, blanch the broccoli first in boiling salted water for 6 minutes, then drain and pat dry. Carry on with the recipe as above. You'll still get the sesame flavour and dressing, just without the char if that's not your thing.

# Coconut Lime Leaf Curry + Tofu, Hispi Cabbage + Coconut Rice

Ve / DF / GF (use gluten-free soy)

This is hands down one of the best sauces to ever come out of Farmer J. It started with turkey meatballs, and honestly, they were outrageous. Then we threw it on tofu, and we've not looked back since. I want to swear, but I won't – it's that good. Think punchy, creamy, sweet-sour magic with lime leaves and fresh chilli coating crispy tofu and roasted cabbage. Add coconut rice, fresh herbs and a shower of sesame, and you've got yourself one ridiculously delicious bowl of food.

**SERVES 4–6**
**PREP TIME: 30 MINS (PLUS MARINATING)**
**COOK TIME: 40–50 MINS**

## INGREDIENTS

FOR THE TOFU & CABBAGE
- 400g firm or semi-firm tofu, cut into cubes
- 1 hispi cabbage, roughly chopped (or use red cabbage)
- 2 tbsp sesame seeds (mix of black and white)
- 2 tbsp chopped fresh coriander
- 2 spring onions, chopped

FOR THE LIME LEAF BASE SAUCE
- 3–4 fresh red chillies
- Juice of 4 limes
- 1 tsp chilli flakes
- 8 fresh lime leaves
- 90g (6 tbsp) tomato purée
- 1 tbsp salt
- 2 tbsp ground turmeric
- 1 tbsp peeled and grated fresh turmeric
- 2 tbsp soft light brown sugar
- 2 tbsp grated fresh ginger
- 7–8 garlic cloves
- 5 tbsp soy sauce
- 235ml water
- 235ml neutral oil (such as avocado, pomace or sunflower oil)

FOR THE COCONUT-LIME SAUCE
(Made from the base, this becomes your marinade, roasting sauce and finishing drizzle.)
- 250g Lime Leaf Base Sauce (see above)
- 400ml tin Thai coconut milk
- 1½ tbsp soy sauce

FOR THE COCONUT RICE
- 200g jasmine rice
- 400ml tin Thai coconut milk
- 235ml water

**METHOD**

**1.** First, make the lime leaf base sauce. Blitz the chillies, lime juice, chilli flakes, lime leaves, tomato purée, salt, both types of turmeric, brown sugar, ginger, garlic, soy sauce and water until smooth. Stir in the oil. This is your master base, bold, citrusy and spiced.

**2.** Now make the coconut-lime sauce. Scoop 250g of the base into a bowl. Store the rest in the fridge for up to a week. Whisk in the coconut milk and soy sauce. Taste it. It should be punchy, sharp, savoury and rich.

**3.** Press your tofu between kitchen paper to draw out excess moisture, ideally for a few hours. Toss in two-thirds of the coconut-lime sauce and marinate for at least 30 minutes. More time = more flavour.

**4.** Preheat the oven to 200°C fan (220°C/425°F). Spread the tofu on a baking tray lined with baking parchment and roast for 20–25 minutes until golden and crisp at the edges.

**5.** Rinse the jasmine rice until the water runs clear. Tip into a saucepan with the coconut milk, water and a pinch of salt. Bring to the boil, then cover and simmer for 15–18 minutes. Fluff with a fork.

**6.** Transfer the tofu to a large cast-iron pan or roasting tray with the chopped cabbage. Add a generous glug of the coconut-lime sauce, toss, and roast for 10 minutes so everything gets sticky and charred.

**7.** Pour over the remaining coconut-lime sauce and return to the oven for a final 5 minutes, just to warm through.

**8.** To serve, spoon the tofu and cabbage mix over the coconut rice. Drizzle with any pan juices and top with sesame seeds, chopped coriander and spring onion. Serve hot and make sure every forkful gets a bit of everything.

SESAME SEEDS

# Smashed Cucumber Salad + Miso Tahini Ponzu Dressing

Ve / GF (use gluten-free soy sauce) / DF

This one's a fresh, crunchy, salty-sour hit. Smashed cucumbers soak up all the punchy dressing, made creamy with a bit of tahini and miso for body and depth. It's everything we want in a side dish: zingy, bold and full of texture thanks to sesame seeds and nori. Serve it with grilled fish, sticky rice, or just eat it straight from the bowl with your hands (we won't judge).
(Image overleaf, with Green Za'atar Shakshuka (pae 61))

**SERVES 3–4**
**PREP TIME: 20 MINS**

## INGREDIENTS

- 10–12 Persian or Lebanese cucumbers (about 600g)
- 1 small red onion, thinly sliced
- 50g fresh coriander, chopped
- 10 fresh mint leaves, torn
- 2 tbsp toasted sesame seeds (mix of white and black)
- 25g nori flakes
- Sea salt and black pepper

FOR THE MISO TAHINI PONZU DRESSING
- Juice of 1 lemon
- 3 tbsp soy sauce
- 1 tbsp white miso
- 1 tbsp tahini
- 1 tbsp maple syrup
- 1 tbsp mirin
- 1 garlic clove, grated
- 1 tsp fresh ginger, grated
- 1 tsp chilli flakes (optional)
- 2 good glugs of olive oil
- 2 tsp toasted sesame oil

## METHOD

**1.** Give the cucumbers a rinse, then smash them gently with the flat side of a big knife or a rolling pin until they crack and split but still hold together. Chop into bite-sized chunks, sprinkle with sea salt and let them sit for 5–10 minutes to draw out the water. Rinse briefly, then pat dry. Set aside.

**2.** Whisk together all the ingredients for the dressing, then taste and tweak as needed. It should be zingy, punchy and sharp.

**3.** In a big bowl, toss the smashed cucumbers with the sliced red onion, chopped coriander and torn mint. Pour over the dressing and toss gently to coat the cucumber. Add more dressing if you like, then finish with a generous handful of toasted sesame seeds and nori flakes. Add a final pinch of salt and black pepper. Eat straight away while it's vibrant and crunchy, or chill it in the fridge for 15–20 minutes to let the flavours settle in.

# Sesame Milk Bun Bagels
Ve / DF

Soft, fluffy, sesame-coated beauties – these are not your classic bagel. We keep it stripped back and vegan-friendly: no eggs, no dairy, just good olive oil and creamy plant milk doing the heavy lifting. Straight out of the oven, golden and warm, they smell like every bakery you've ever loved. Load them up with labneh, za'atar, hard-boiled eggs or falafel (or just go for all three). Proper comfort food. (Image overleaf)

**MAKES 8 BAGELS**
**PREP TIME: 2½ HOURS (INCLUDING PROVING AND SHAPING)**
**COOK TIME: 15 MINS**

### INGREDIENTS
- 300ml oat milk or other plant-based milk
- 20g fresh yeast or 7g active dried yeast
- 500g bread flour
- 10g caster sugar
- 12g fine sea salt
- 40ml olive or pomace oil
- Sesame seeds (white), for topping

### OPTIONAL TOPPINGS
- Za'atar
- Poppy seeds
- Dried herbs

### METHOD

**1.** Pour the milk into a pan and warm just a little over a very low heat – do not boil it – then dissolve the yeast in it and leave it for 5 minutes until it bubbles like it's coming to life.

**2.** Into a stand mixer fitted with a dough hook, add the milk-yeast mix, flour, sugar, salt and oil. Mix on low speed for 4–5 minutes until it all comes together, then bump it up to medium and knead for another 4–5 minutes until it's smooth and stretchy.

**3.** Scoop the dough into a lightly oiled bowl, cover it with a clean tea towel, and let it rest for 30 minutes. Then give it a few folds, pull the dough from one side, fold it over, rotate the bowl, repeat. This doesn't need to be perfect; you just want to give it some structure. Let it rest again for another 30 minutes.

**4.** Cut the dough into eight equal pieces and roll each one into a smooth ball. Rest them for 15 minutes on a baking tray covered with a tea towel to relax the gluten – this will make them easier to shape.

**5.** Flatten each ball slightly, roll it into a chunky sausage and bring the ends together to form a bagel. Press the seam gently to seal. Dip each one quickly in cold water, then roll them in sesame seeds or your topping of choice. Line them up on a baking tray lined with baking parchment, cover loosely with cling film, and let them prove for 45 minutes until puffed.

**6.** Towards the end of the proving time, preheat the oven to 180°C fan (200°C/400°F). Bake the bagels for 15 minutes until golden and crisp on the outside. Let them cool on a wire rack.

**SESAME SEEDS**

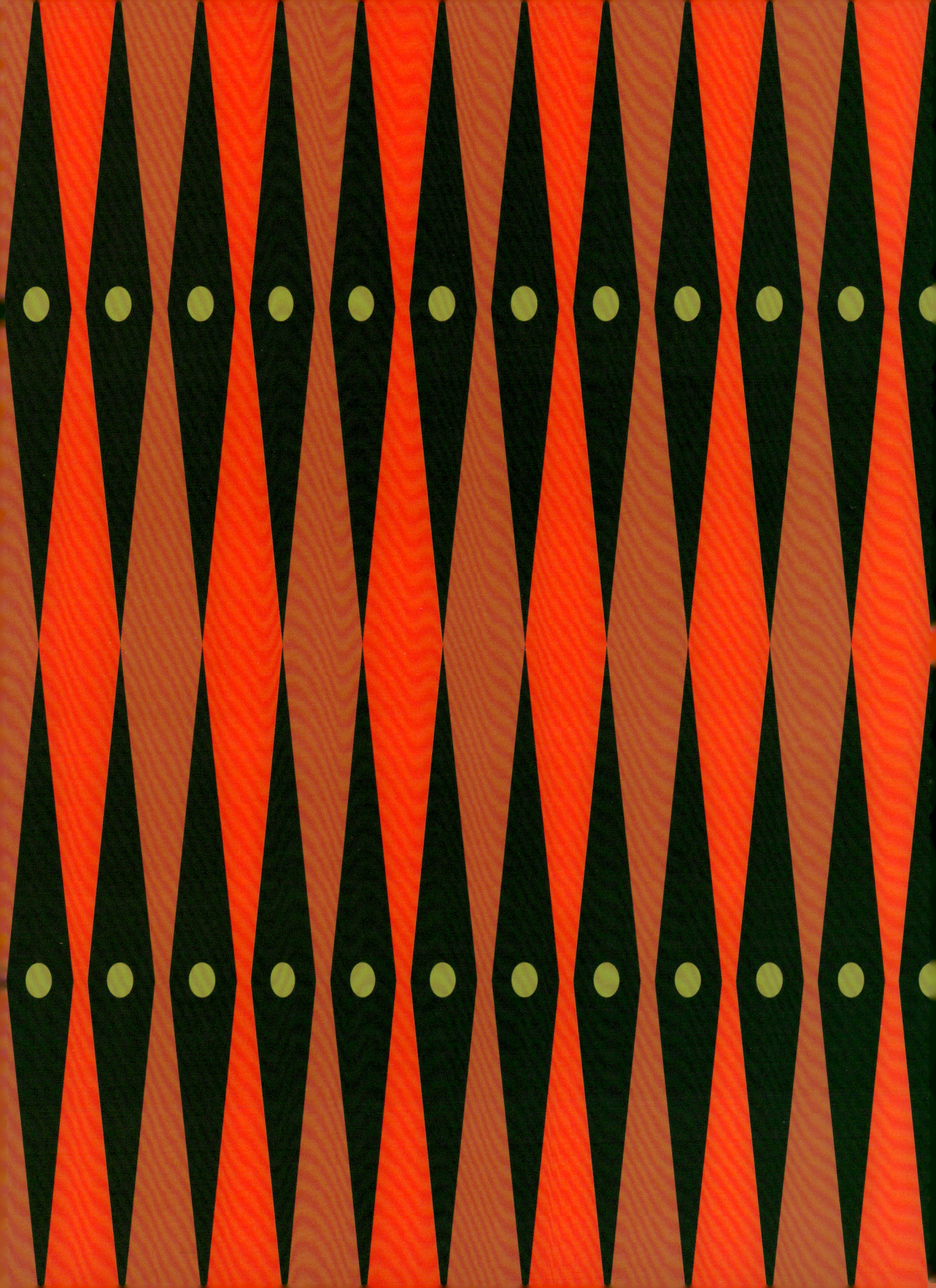

# PICKLES & Ferments

| Pickled Chilli/ Red Onion | Kalamata Olives | Preserved Lemon | Gochujang |
|---|---|---|---|
| *160* | *166* | *174* | *184* |

# Pickled Chilli & Pickled Red Onion

*your go-to flavour finishers*

---

We nearly gave each of these their own section because honestly, they deserve it. But we had to compromise somewhere. These two flavour finishers live side-by-side in the fridge, so they can go side-by-side here.

Pickled chilli is a bit of a stealth weapon. It's got heat but not the kind that blows your head off; just the right hum. It adds depth and fire to anything. Pickled red onion, on the other hand, is the fresh slap of acid every dish needs – it's tangy, crunchy and downright addictive. Tossed through salads, stuffed in wraps or piled on toast, it makes everything taste brighter, sharper, better.

And a quick word on pickling vs fermenting, because they're not the same thing. Pickling is all about acid. You dunk your veg in vinegar or a briny solution, and boom, they're preserved – quick, sharp and zero fuss. Fermenting, on the other hand, is slower and funkier. It relies on natural bacteria to do their thing, bringing probiotics and deeper umami flavour to the party. Pickled = fast and zingy. Fermented = slow and complex. Both are great, just different.

# Pickled Chilli Aioli

DF

This one's creamy, punchy and spicy. It's the aioli we reach for when grilled meats are involved, when veg needs a little something, or when we're dunking chips and pretending it's just a snack.

**MAKES ABOUT 250ML**
**PREP TIME: 10 MINS**

### INGREDIENTS

- 30g pickled hot chillies (any good jarred kind will do)
- 2 garlic cloves, grated
- 4 egg yolks
- 1 tbsp (about 15g) Dijon mustard
- 125ml neutral oil (such as avocado, pomace or sunflower oil)
- 125ml extra virgin olive oil
- 1 tbsp white wine vinegar
- A few drops of Worcestershire sauce
- 2-3 drops of Tabasco
- Pinch of salt

### METHOD

**1.** Start by blitzing your pickled chillies and garlic in a small blender or food processor. You want it as smooth as possible as any big chilli bits will mess with the texture.

**2.** Add the egg yolks, mustard and your chilli-garlic paste to a tall container or bowl. Use a hand-held stick blender to blitz until combined and starting to thicken. Very slowly, drizzle in the oils while blending continuously, a trickle at first, then more once it starts to emulsify. Keep going until you've added both oils and your aioli is thick, glossy and holding its shape. Add the vinegar, Worcestershire sauce, Tabasco and salt. Blend again and taste and adjust the seasoning: more vinegar for tang, more chilli for fire, more salt if it's flat.

**3.** Stick it in the fridge until needed, where it will keep for 3 days. Spoon on to everything and try not to eat it straight out of the jar.

# Quick Pickled Red Onion

Ve / GF / DF

Quick pickled red onions are a fridge essential. Sharp, punchy, and ready to liven up whatever you're eating. Throw them on eggs, salads, sandwiches ... anything that needs a bit of tang.

**MAKES 1 LARGE JAR (ABOUT 400ML)**
**PREP TIME: 10 MINS**
**PICKLING TIME: 4–24 HOURS**

### INGREDIENTS

- 3 red onions, thinly sliced (about 3mm thick)
- 100ml red wine vinegar
- 100ml water
- 2 tbsp sugar
- 1 tsp fine salt

### METHOD

**1.** Start by getting the onions thinly sliced and into a clean jar or container.

**2.** In a small pan, combine the red wine vinegar, water, sugar and salt. Warm gently over a low heat until everything's dissolved (give it a stir) and take it off the heat to cool slightly. Pour the warm brine over the onions so they're completely submerged.

**3.** Seal the jar and stick it in the fridge for 4–24 hours. These will keep in the fridge for up to 2 weeks.

# Leche de Tigre Ceviche + Pickled Red Onion

GF / DF

Leche de tigre, which translates as 'tiger's milk', is a punchy, citrus-based sauce from Peru, traditionally used to marinate ceviche. It's bright, spicy and full of flavour: zingy lime, fresh ginger and a slap of red onion, all blitzed into a sharp, savoury liquid that 'cooks' your fish in minutes. We serve it our way: chunks of fresh ceviche bathed in the leche, topped with tangy pickled onions, a spoon of sweet potato purée for creaminess, and a crunch of crispy corn on top.

**SERVES 2**
**PREP TIME: 20 MINS**
**COOK TIME: 30 MINS**

### INGREDIENTS

FOR THE CEVICHE
- 200–300g fresh thick fish fillets (bass, snapper, or any firm white fish), skinned and cubed
- 2 tbsp Quick Pickled Red Onion (page 161)
- Handful of shop-bought crispy corn kernels (look for them as 'giant corn' or 'cancha' in Latin American shops; any crunchy, salty corn will do)
- A few coriander leaves

FOR THE LECHE DE TIGRE
- 2.5cm piece of fresh ginger, peeled
- Juice of 6–8 limes
- ½ celery stick, roughly chopped
- 2 red onions, roughly chopped
- 100–150ml cold water
- Sea salt and black pepper

FOR THE SWEET POTATO PURÉE
- 2 sweet potatoes (about 250g), peeled and chopped
- 2 tbsp olive oil

### METHOD

**1.** Start by roasting the sweet potatoes at 200°C fan (220°C/425°F) for 25–30 minutes until soft. Tip into a food processor with the olive oil and a pinch of salt and blitz to a smooth purée.

**2.** Move on to your leche de tigre. Blend the ginger, lime juice, celery and onions until smooth. Gradually add the water to loosen it – how much depends on how punchy you want it. Season well.

**3.** In a bowl, season the cubed fish with salt and pepper, pour the leche de tigre over, mix gently and let it sit for 3–5 minutes max. Any longer and your fish will go mushy.

**4.** Now you're ready to plate. Add a big swoosh of sweet potato purée to each of two shallow bowls. Spoon your marinated fish into the bowls and top with a good tangle of pickled red onions and a scatter of crispy corn. Finish with coriander leaves.

PICKLED CHILLI & PICKLED RED ONION

# Shaved Winter Greens + Coriander Vinaigrette

Ve / GF (use gluten-free soy sauce) / DF

We love a crunchy salad and this one's all about crisp greens, bright herbs and that coriander vinaigrette. It cuts through like a knife and brings everything to life.

**SERVES 4**
**PREP TIME: 15 MINS**

## INGREDIENTS
- 100g white cabbage, shredded
- 100g Brussels sprouts, shredded
- 50g green beans, topped, tailed and blanched
- 25g Quick Pickled Red Onion (page 161)
- 10g fresh coriander, chopped
- 5–6 mint leaves, torn

FOR THE CORIANDER VINAIGRETTE (MAKES ABOUT 200ML)
- 125ml neutral oil (such as avocado, pomace or sunflower oil)
- Juice of 1 large lemon (about 60ml)
- 2 tbsp toasted sesame oil
- 1½ tbsp soy sauce
- 1½ tsp sea salt
- 1 garlic clove, grated
- 1 tsp Dijon mustard
- 12g fresh coriander, chopped

## METHOD

**1.** Throw all the ingredients for the vinaigrette into a blender and blitz until smooth and bright green. It should taste sharp, nutty and herby.

**2.** Add the shredded cabbage, sprouts, blanched green beans, pickled red onion, coriander and mint leaves to a large bowl. Drizzle over about 4-5 tablespoons of the coriander vinaigrette and toss it all together (the remaining vinaigrette will keep in the fridge for 1 week).

**3.** Give it a quick taste, and add a pinch of salt, an extra squeeze of lemon or another splash of dressing if it needs a lift. Plate it high.

# Pickled Chilli Chickpea Salad

Ve / GF / DF

Crispy za'atar chickpeas. Shredded cabbage. Pickled chilli. And then that sharp, creamy lemon tahini dressing. This one hits them all – crunchy, herby, spicy and tangy.

**SERVES 2–3**
**PREP TIME: 20 MINS**
**COOK TIME: 7 MINS**

## INGREDIENTS

- 400g tin chickpeas, rinsed and drained
- 1 tbsp olive oil
- 1 tsp za'atar
- ¼ tsp sea salt
- 150g white cabbage, finely shredded
- 150g Lebanese cucumbers (about 2 small ones), halved and sliced
- 150g green pepper (1 small one), deseeded and sliced
- 50g pickled green chilli
- 40g Quick Pickled Red Onion (page 161)
- 80g Pickled Cucumber (page 146), sliced
- Bunch of flat-leaf parsley, leaves chopped
- ½ tsp sumac

FOR THE LEMON TAHINI DRESSING
- 80g tahini
- 3 tbsp olive oil
- 2 tbsp lemon juice
- ½ tsp salt
- ¼ tsp ground cumin

## METHOD

**1.** Preheat the oven to 200°C fan (220°C/425°F). Toss the chickpeas with the olive oil, za'atar and salt, spread out on a baking tray and roast for 7 minutes until crispy and golden. Let them cool a little while you prepare the dressing.

**2.** In a bowl, whisk together the tahini, olive oil, lemon juice, salt and cumin. Add a splash of water to thin it out if needed – it should pour but still coat a spoon.

**3.** Add the cabbage, cucumbers, green pepper, pickled chilli, pickled red onion, pickled cucumber and most of the parsley to a large serving bowl. Give it all a good toss, then add the warm za'atar chickpeas. Pour over the lemon tahini dressing and toss again to coat everything evenly. Finish with a handful of fresh parsley and a good sprinkle of sumac.

**4.** Serve it straight away, while the chickpeas are still crunchy.

# Kalamata Olives

*Jonathan's obsession*

---

Jonathan's obsession with kalamata olives is . . . intense. We've had to pull him back more than once. If it were up to him, he'd toss a handful into every single dish – breakfast, lunch or dinner. And while we admire the commitment, we had to draw the line somewhere.

But rant aside, we get it. Kalamata olives really *are* something special. They've got that rich, fruity, slightly smoky flavour with just enough saltiness to cut through and make other ingredients shine. They're meaty, satisfying and have a depth that's hard to beat; one olive is enough to transform a bite of veg, cheese or grain into something way more interesting. They bring oomph without overpowering, which is no small feat.

They're also incredibly versatile: whether chopped into a salad, stirred through a pasta, or baked into focaccia, they just work. That hit of briny, savoury goodness lifts everything around it. And unlike some ingredients that fade into the background, kalamatas know how to hold their own. Maybe Jonathan's not completely wrong after all . . .

# Kalamata Gilda

GF / DF (without feta)

This is honestly the first thing Jonathan does when he lands in Spain. No suitcase, no suncream, just heads straight for the nearest bar and grabs a *gilda*. It's salty, punchy, unapologetic. And it's basically a skewer of some of our favourite things: kalamata olives (of course), anchovies and sharp little pickled peppers. Perfect for a drinks party or handing round at a celebration. A heavenly start to the night, or day.
(Image on page 78, top)

**MAKES 8 (TO SERVE 4)**
**PREP TIME: 10 MINS**

### INGREDIENTS
- 16 kalamata olives, pitted
- 8 anchovy fillets in oil
- 8 pickled guindilla peppers (or mild green pickled chillies)
- 8 cubes of feta cheese (optional)
- Extra virgin olive oil, for drizzling
- Zest of 1 lemon (optional)
- Sea salt and black pepper

### METHOD

**1.** Grab eight small wooden skewers. Start with a kalamata olive, then an anchovy (fold it if it's long), then a guindilla pepper. If you're going the feta route, now's the time to slide on a cube. Finish with another kalamata olive. Repeat until you've got eight skewers lined up like proud little flavour soldiers.

**2.** Drizzle each one with a bit of good olive oil. Add a pinch of lemon zest (if using) and season lightly with salt and black pepper (the anchovies and olives bring their own salt, so go easy). You can let them sit in the fridge for 30 minutes.

**KALAMATA OLIVES**

# Farmer J Nicoise

GF / DF

If Jonathan had it his way, every salad would have kalamata olives in it. But for me? Every salad would have tuna it. So this is my favourite salad. Has been my entire life. Tinned tuna is my ride or die, but fine, we've included an optional seared tuna upgrade if you're trying to impress someone.

Make this for lunch, a dinner party starter, or just eat it straight out of the bowl standing up in your kitchen.

**SERVES 2–4**
**PREP TIME: 30 MINS**
**COOK TIME: 15 MINS**

### INGREDIENTS
- 250g baby potatoes (about 15)
- 100g green beans
- 3 eggs
- 1 fresh 250–300g tuna steak (or use really good-quality tinned tuna, like Ortiz)
- Olive oil, for brushing
- 2 heads of Belgian (white) endive, sliced
- 1 head of red endive, sliced
- ½ cos lettuce, torn
- 1–2 baby gem lettuces, quartered
- 1 sweet pointed red (Romano) pepper, thinly sliced
- 50g kalamata olives, whole or halved
- 150g Nicoise dressing (recipe below)
- 4–6 anchovies (optional)
- Sea salt and black pepper

### FOR THE NICOISE DRESSING
- Juice of 1 lemon
- 25ml white wine vinegar
- 1 tbsp Dijon mustard
- 2 anchovy fillets
- ½ tsp honey
- 1 garlic clove, grated
- 5 tbsp olive oil

### METHOD

**1.** Cook the potatoes in boiling salted water until tender, then drain and halve when cool enough to handle. Blanch the green beans and refresh in iced water.

**2.** Hard-boil the eggs in boiling water for about 7 minutes; you are looking for a jammy centre. Transfer into a bowl of iced water or run under cold water for a few minutes.

**3.** Make the dressing by blending the lemon juice, vinegar, mustard, anchovies, honey and garlic until smooth. Slowly drizzle in the oil while blending until it thickens into a creamy, punchy vinaigrette. Season with salt and pepper and set aside.

**4.** Rub the tuna with a bit of oil and season with salt and pepper. Sear in a very hot pan for 30–45 seconds on each side, just to get some colour. Leave it raw and ruby red in the middle. Leave to rest for a couple of minutes, then thinly slice.

**5.** In a large, shallow serving bowl, arrange the endives, cos, baby gem, sliced pepper and olives with the potatoes and green beans. Season with salt and pepper and pour over a generous glug of the dressing. Peel and halve the eggs, then add to the top of the salad with the anchovies (if using) and seared tuna slices. Yum.

**KALAMATA OLIVES**

# Heritage Tomato + Kalamata Panzanella

V

This is sunshine in a bowl, even if it's pouring outside. Juicy heritage tomatoes, preferably Isle of Wight, salty kalamatas, sharp preserved lemon and crunchy pitta chips soaking up a rich, punchy dressing.

**SERVES 4–6**
**PREP TIME: 25 MINS**

### INGREDIENTS
- 1.2kg heritage tomatoes
- 250g cavolo nero, torn and washed
- 600g sweet pointed red (Romano) peppers, thinly sliced
- 150g kalamata olives, pitted
- 10g green chillies, thinly sliced
- 120g Preserved Lemon (page 175), finely diced
- 250g Pitta Chips (page 125)
- 150g feta cheese, crumbled
- Sea salt

FOR THE DRESSING
- 50g kalamata olives, pitted
- 1½ tbsp good-quality balsamic vinegar
- Juice of 1 lemon
- 2 garlic cloves, grated
- 1 tbsp Dijon mustard
- 10g sea salt
- 100ml olive oil

### METHOD

**1.** Slice the tomatoes into nice big chunks or wedges, sprinkle with a pinch of salt and leave them in a large bowl for 10 minutes so they start to release their juices. This is where the magic begins.

**2.** Meanwhile, make the dressing. In a blender or food processor, blitz the kalamata olives, balsamic vinegar, lemon juice, garlic, mustard and salt. Slowly stream in the olive oil until it emulsifies to make a rich, salty vinaigrette. Set aside.

**3.** Once the tomatoes have softened slightly, toss in the cavolo nero, red peppers, olives, green chillies and preserved lemon. Add the pitta chips last so they stay crunchy but start to soak up a bit of the tomato juice and dressing. Drizzle over the kalamata dressing and toss gently. You want everything coated but still holding shape, no mush.

**4.** Transfer to a serving platter and scatter over the feta crumbs. Serve immediately while it's all still full of crunch and colour.

KALAMATA OLIVES

# Cavolo Nero, Butter Beans, Kalamata + Oregano Salad

Ve / GF / DF

Creamy butter beans meet crunchy greens and salty olives in this herby little number. The beans are soft and satisfying, almost silky, and the cavolo – well, that stuff needs a proper massage if you're serving it raw. A quick rub with a bit of dressing softens it right up and brings out its flavour. This salad's all about contrast: rich and sharp, tender and crisp, fresh and punchy. Serve it solo, pack it for lunch, or throw it down next to something hot off the grill.

**SERVES 2 AS A MAIN OR 4 AS A SIDE**
**PREP TIME: 20 MINS**

## INGREDIENTS

- 50g cavolo nero, torn or roughly shredded
- 200g tinned butter beans or kidney beans, rinsed and drained (or use any good-quality bean)
- 50g kalamata olives, pitted and halved
- 150g cherry tomatoes, halved
- 20g sun-dried tomatoes, roughly chopped
- 1 small red onion, thinly sliced
- 50g fresh flat-leaf parsley, chopped
- 50g fresh coriander, chopped
- 10g fresh oregano, chopped

FOR THE OREGANO DRESSING
- 70ml extra virgin olive oil
- 2 tbsp lemon juice
- 1 tbsp sherry vinegar
- 1 tsp Dijon mustard
- 1 garlic clove, grated
- 1 tbsp dried oregano
- 1 tsp sea salt
- 1 tsp freshly ground black pepper

## METHOD

**1.** First make the dressing. Whisk together the olive oil, lemon juice, sherry vinegar, mustard, garlic, dried oregano, salt and pepper until emulsified and full of zing.

**2.** If you're using tough cavolo, give it a 2-minute blanch in boiling water, then refresh in iced water and pat dry. Otherwise, keep it raw and rugged. Throw the cavolo nero into a large bowl and pour in a tablespoon of the dressing. Massage thoroughly with your hands to soften it up.

**3.** Add all the remaining salad ingredients to the bowl, then pour over the dressing. Toss gently; don't smash the beans. Taste and adjust the seasoning if needed, and serve it up.

KALAMATA OLIVES

# Preserved Lemon

*sharp, salty and rich*

---

Preserved lemon is one of those ingredients that sneaks unexpectedly into breakfast, lunch and dinner at Farmer J. It's sharp, salty and rich with citrus oils that have mellowed and fermented into something much deeper. You can't quite put your finger on it when it's in a dish, but you know it's what's making everything taste better. It doesn't shout, it hums in the background, bringing all the other flavours into tune.

Now, we've had some absolutely banging preserved lemons over the years and some that tasted like someone dropped a bar of soap into a jar of vinegar. Honestly, if it's bitter and weirdly perfumed, what's the point? That's why we started making our own. When it's done right, preserved lemon has this almost buttery texture, and the rind (which is the bit you use) becomes the hero: soft, fragrant and packed with flavour.

Buy the good stuff if you can find it, but better yet, make your own. We've given you two ways to do it: the long road (proper, old-school, fermented) and a quick cheat's version when you just can't wait. Both are good, both will elevate your cooking, and both will make you wonder how you ever cooked without it. Keep a jar in the fridge and thank us later.

# Proper Preserved Lemons

Ve / GF / DF

Proper preserved lemons, done the old-school way, with salt, time and a little love. Fermentation brings out that deep, mellow tang you just can't rush. Once you've got a jar on the go, you'll be chucking these into everything.

**MAKES 1 LARGE JAR (ABOUT 1 LITRE)**
**PREP TIME: 20 MINS**
**FERMENTATION TIME: 3–4 WEEKS**

### INGREDIENTS
- 3kg organic lemons (thin-skinned if you can get them)
- 500g sea salt
- Black pepper
- A few sprigs of fresh thyme
- 2–3 dried chillies (optional)
- Extra lemon juice (if needed, to top up)
- 120ml olive oil (to seal the top)

### METHOD
1. Give the lemons a good scrub, then dry them. Slice them into thin rounds, about 3–4mm thick. You want the salt to get right in there, so don't make them too chunky.

2. Grab a big sterilised jar and start layering. Lemons first, then a generous sprinkle of salt, a few grinds of black pepper, a sprig of thyme, and a chilli if you're using them. Press it all down with your hands or the back of a spoon. Keep layering until the jar is nearly full, pressing as you go. You want the juice to start releasing; this is key. Once you've packed it all in, press down hard one more time.

3. Seal the jar and leave it at room temperature for 5 days. Check it daily; if the lemons aren't submerged in their own juice after the 5 days, top up with fresh lemon juice to cover them completely. Then pour a layer of olive oil over the top – this keeps the air out and stops anything funky from creeping in.

4. Seal again. Now the waiting begins. Leave it in a cool, dark cupboard for 3–4 weeks. When it's done, the rind should be soft and the whole thing deeply fragrant. Once opened, keep it in the fridge for up to 3 weeks and use a clean spoon to scoop from the jar.

# Quick Preserved Lemons

Ve / GF / DF

Can't wait a month? This is your speedy fix – not as funky as the long version, but still bright, salty and full of citrus punch.

**MAKES 1 JAR**
**PREP TIME: 10 MINS**
**FRIDGE TIME: 24 HOURS**

### INGREDIENTS
- 1.2kg organic lemons
- 30g fine sea salt (or 2.5 per cent of lemon weight)

### METHOD
1. Wash and dry the lemons. Slice into rounds, then quarter each round, removing seeds as you go. Toss with the salt until well coated. Pack into a sterilised jar, pressing down to release the juice. Seal and chill in the fridge. Ready in 24 hours.

# Avocado Toast
# + Preserved Lemon, Chilli & Coriander

Ve / DF

Yes, yes, we know. Avo toast. Groundbreaking. Don't hate us for it. But as one of our most popular breakfast dishes at Farmer J, we had to spill the beans. What makes ours special? That salty, citrusy hit of preserved lemon. It cuts through all that creamy avo and turns a good toast into a bloody brilliant one.

**SERVES 2**
**PREP TIME: 10 MINS**
**COOK TIME: 2–3 MINS**

### INGREDIENTS
- 2 ripe avocados
- 2 slices of good sourdough (or whatever bread you like), toasted
- 1 tbsp Preserved Lemon (page 175), finely chopped
- ¼ tsp chilli flakes (more if you like heat)
- Handful of fresh coriander, chopped
- Extra virgin olive oil, for drizzling
- Squeeze of lemon juice (optional)
- Sea salt and black pepper

### METHOD

**1.** Halve the avocados, ditch the stones and scoop the flesh into a bowl. Cut into big chunks – no mashing. You want those creamy cubes. Stir gently to break it up just a little, keeping plenty of texture.

**2.** Spoon the avocado on to the toast, scatter over the preserved lemon, chilli flakes and coriander, season generously and finish with a glug of good olive oil and a squeeze of lemon juice, if you want some extra zing.

# Herb Frittata + Preserved Lemon + Feta

V

A frittata is one of those anytime dishes; it works for breakfast, lunch or a quick dinner. But this one is different. Serve it with labneh on the side – technically optional, but as far as we're concerned, not really.
(Image overleaf)

**SERVES 4**
**PREP TIME: 10 MINS**
**COOK TIME: 20 MINS**

### INGREDIENTS
- 1–2 tbsp olive oil
- ½ onion, diced
- 8 large eggs
- 125ml milk (or cream, for extra richness)
- 25g fresh parsley, chopped
- 12g fresh coriander, chopped
- 100g feta cheese, crumbled
- 1 heaped tbsp finely chopped Preserved Lemon (page 175)
- 1 tbsp butter (optional)
- Sea salt and black pepper

FOR THE LABNEH DIP
- 200g Labneh (page 40)
- 1 heaped tbsp finely chopped Preserved Lemon (page 175)
- 2 tbsp olive oil
- 1 tbsp lemon juice
- 4 tbsp chopped chives

### METHOD

**1.** Preheat the oven to 180°C fan (200°C/400°F).

**2.** Heat 1 tablespoon of the olive oil in an ovenproof pan (25cm works well) over a medium heat, add the diced onion and cook for 3–4 minutes until soft. While that's going, crack the eggs into a bowl and whisk with the milk, a pinch of salt and pepper, parsley, coriander, most of the crumbled feta and the preserved lemon. Stir it all together.

**3.** Add a little more oil to the pan, if needed, and pour the egg mixture over the softened onion. Let it cook gently for a couple of minutes until it starts to set around the edges. Dot the top with the rest of the feta and, if you're into richness, a knob of butter.

**4.** Slide the pan into the oven and cook for 12–15 minutes until just set and golden on top.

**5.** While it's baking, make the dip. Mix the labneh with the preserved lemon, olive oil and lemon juice. Season to taste with salt and pepper and scatter over the chives.

**6.** Serve slices of the frittata straight from the pan, cooled to room temperature or from the fridge, with dollops of labneh on the side. This also works well with a spoonful of schug if you've got some knocking about. The Harissa Fennel Salad (page 42) is a great accompaniment to cut through the richness.

**PRESERVED LEMON**

# Preserved Lemon, Chickpea, Spinach + Swiss Chard Stew

Ve (without yoghurt, feta or labneh) / GF / DF

There's no better bowl on a rainy day. It's earthy from the chickpeas, bright from the preserved lemon, and full of green from spinach and Swiss chard. This is one of those 'scoop with a spoon and mop with bread' kind of stews. The preserved lemon brings the whole thing to life: rich and tangy, yet sharp enough to cut through the comfort. Optional extras like feta work a treat, but it's solid on its own.

**SERVES 3–4**
**PREP TIME: 10 MINS**
**COOK TIME: 25 MINS**

### INGREDIENTS
- 2 tbsp olive oil
- 1 onion, diced
- 2 garlic cloves, grated
- 1 tsp cumin seeds
- 1 tsp coriander seeds
- 1 tsp ground turmeric
- 400g tin or jar chickpeas, drained and rinsed
- 475ml vegetable stock (or water)
- 120g fresh spinach, chopped
- 60g Swiss chard, chopped
- 1 tbsp chopped Preserved Lemon (page 175)
- Juice of ½ lemon
- 1 tbsp chopped fresh parsley
- 1 tbsp chopped fresh coriander
- Sea salt and black pepper

### TO SERVE
- Warm flatbread or rice
- Yoghurt, labneh or feta (optional)
- Drizzle of extra virgin olive oil (optional)

### METHOD
**1.** Start by heating the olive oil in a large saucepan over a medium heat. Add the diced onion and cook for 5–7 minutes until soft. Stir in the garlic, cumin seeds, coriander seeds and turmeric and cook for another minute or two until everything smells warm and toasty.

**2.** Tip in the chickpeas, give it all a good stir, then pour in the vegetable stock. Bring it up to a simmer and let it bubble away for 10 minutes so the chickpeas soak up all that spiced flavour. Stir in the spinach, Swiss chard, and the preserved lemon. Let the greens wilt down for 5–7 minutes until tender but still bright.

**3.** Season with salt and pepper; if you fancy more zing, a squeeze of lemon juice never hurts. Spoon into bowls, then finish with chopped parsley and coriander.

**4.** Serve with warm flatbread or rice. Add a dollop of yoghurt, labneh or some crumbled feta and a swirl of good olive oil to make it even more indulgent.

# Charred Courgette, Preserved Lemon, Mint + Pine Nuts

V / GF

This is one of those outrageously simple sides that punches well above its weight. You've got smoky courgettes, zippy preserved lemon, fresh mint and toasted pine nuts doing their thing. It's bright, fresh, a bit luxurious and somehow still low-effort. Stick it next to grilled chicken, serve it on toast with some whipped feta, or simply pile it on to a plate. It'll never let you down.

**SERVES 4**
**PREP TIME: 10 MINS**
**COOK TIME: 10–20 MINS**

## INGREDIENTS

- 2 tbsp pine nuts
- 4 courgettes, sliced lengthways into thick 1–1.5cm strips
- 3 tbsp olive oil
- 1 heaped tbsp chopped Preserved Lemon (page 175)
- 1 tbsp lemon juice
- Small bunch of fresh mint, leaves roughly chopped
- Crumbled feta or goat's cheese, to finish (optional)
- Sea salt and black pepper

## METHOD

**1.** Toast the pine nuts in a dry frying pan over a medium heat, shaking often until golden and fragrant. Watch them like a hawk: they go from golden to burnt in a flash.

**2.** Heat a griddle pan or barbecue to medium-high while you toss the courgette strips with 2 tablespoons of the olive oil and some salt and pepper. Get them on to the grill and cook for 3–4 minutes each side until nicely charred but still holding their shape. If you are using a griddle pan you might need to do this in two batches. Set aside to cool slightly.

**3.** In a small bowl, mix the preserved lemon with the lemon juice, the remaining tablespoon of olive oil and most of the chopped mint (reserve a little to garnish). Season to taste with salt and pepper – it should be tangy and punchy.

**4.** Lay the courgette strips on a platter, spoon over the lemon and mint dressing, then scatter the toasted pine nuts on top. Finish with more fresh mint and, if you're feeling indulgent, a handful of crumbled feta or goat's cheese.

# Preserved Lemon Tart

V

We love a lemon tart. But this one's got a twist – it's made with our quick preserved lemons. The preserved lemon brings an extra punch: salty, tangy, deeply lemony. Not sharp, not sweet, just perfectly balanced. We've kept the filling creamy and smooth over a classic sweet pastry base.

**SERVES 8–10**
**PREP TIME: 30 MINS (PLUS CHILLING AND SETTING)**
**COOK TIME: 30 MINS**

### INGREDIENTS
FOR THE CRUST
- 200g plain flour
- 50g icing sugar, plus extra for dusting
- Pinch of salt
- 100g cold unsalted butter, cubed
- 1 egg yolk

FOR THE LEMON FILLING
- 3 large eggs
- 150g granulated sugar
- 100g Quick Preserved Lemon (page 175), finely chopped
- 200ml double cream
- Juice of 2 lemons, zest of 1
- 1 tbsp cornflour
- ½ tsp vanilla extract

TO SERVE
- Lime zest (optional)
- 1 lemon, thinly sliced (optional)
- Dollop of crème fraîche
- Fresh seasonal fruit

### METHOD

**1.** In a food processor, pulse together the flour, icing sugar and salt. Add the cold butter and pulse until you have something like breadcrumbs, then drop in the egg yolk and pulse again until it comes together. Add a splash of ice-cold water if it looks a little dry. Tip it on to a clean surface and knead just to bring it into a ball (don't overwork the dough). Wrap in cling film and chill for 30 minutes.

**2.** Roll out the chilled dough to 3mm thick and use it to line a 23cm tart tin. Prick the base with a fork and chill again for 15 minutes.

**3.** Preheat the oven to 180°C fan (200°C/400°F).

**4.** Line the pastry case with baking parchment and baking beans, then blind bake for 10-12 minutes. Remove the parchment and beans and bake for 5-7 more minutes, or until lightly golden. Set aside to cool while you make the filling.

**5.** Whisk the eggs, sugar and chopped preserved lemon together in a bowl. In a pan over a low heat, warm the cream with the lemon juice, zest and cornflour – don't let it boil. Slowly pour the warm cream into the egg mixture while whisking. Pour the whole lot back into the pan and stir over a low heat until thick like custard. Off the heat, stir in the vanilla and let it cool slightly.

**6.** Pour the lemon filling into the cooled tart case and shake gently to level the top. Chill for at least 2 hours until fully set. Dust with icing sugar and grate over a little lime zest (if using) before serving. Decorate with lemon slices if you like, and eat with lashings of crème fraîche and fresh fruit.

PRESERVED LEMON

# Gochujang

*doesn't shout, it smoulders*

---

Thick, deep red and fermented, gochujang is a Korean chilli paste made from soybeans, glutinous rice, red chilli flakes and salt. It's not just spicy, it's sweet, savoury, salty and packed with umami. The kind of heat that builds slowly and lingers in the best way. It's been a staple in Korean cooking for centuries, stirred into stews, slathered on meats, and spooned over rice bowls. And now, it's earned its spot in the Farmer's Pantry.

At Farmer J, we use it like a secret weapon. In glazes, dressings, marinades, sauces and stews. Whisked with vinegar and sesame oil for a fiery salad dressing. Mixed into mayo for a punchy drizzle over corn ribs. Stirred through butter to melt over steak or roast veg. Or lacquered onto salmon, where it caramelises into something sticky, sweet and utterly addictive.

Gochujang doesn't shout – it smoulders. And that's exactly why we love it. Just a spoonful can transform a dish.

# Gochujang Sauce
GF (use gluten-free soy sauce)

This is the Farmer J way of taking a basic shop-bought condiment and making it sing. We love the rich, funky depth of Korean gochujang, but this recipe levels it up with sweet, tangy, nutty and spicy notes that make it seriously addictive. This is the sauce behind our Fieldtray favourite, gochujang sticky salmon and now it's yours. Slather it on salmon, spoon it over rice bowls, drizzle it on roasted veg. Basically, if you've got this in your fridge, dinner's already sorted.

**MAKES 500–600ML**
**PREP TIME: 5–10 MINS**
**COOK TIME (OPTIONAL): 5–7 MINS**

### INGREDIENTS
- 350g shop-bought gochujang
- 100ml soy sauce
- 100ml mirin
- 80ml rice vinegar
- 30g grated fresh ginger or ginger purée
- 20g grated garlic or garlic purée
- 1½ tbsp Dijon mustard
- 1 heaped tbsp tomato purée
- 20ml toasted sesame oil
- 150ml neutral oil (such as avocado, pomace or sunflower oil)
- 20g soft light brown sugar
- 10g sea salt
- 10g gochugaru (or 10g Aleppo pepper or mild chilli flakes)
- 10g garlic granules
- 100ml cold water

### METHOD
**1.** Chuck everything into a bowl; yes, everything. Whisk the hell out of it until smooth, thick and glossy. The oils should emulsify into the mix and turn it into something magical.

**2.** If you want it thicker, pour the whole thing into a pan and simmer over a medium heat for 5–7 minutes. Stir it as it goes; it'll bubble and darken a little, and you'll know it's ready when it coats the back of a spoon. Let it cool completely.

**3.** Pour into a jar and stash in the fridge. It'll keep for 1–2 weeks, but chances are you'll have used it all up long before then.

# Sticky Salmon Rice Bowl
DF

There's something about this bowl that hits every craving. Spicy, sticky salmon glazed in our signature gochujang sauce. Served with creamy smashed avo, coconut rice, crunchy smashed cucumber salad and kale miso slaw. Finish with lime, fresh chilli and a scatter of sesame seeds. It's rich, fresh and properly satisfying.

**SERVES 4**
**PREP TIME: 30 MINS (PLUS MARINATING)**
**COOK TIME: 25 MINS**

### INGREDIENTS
- 4 skinless salmon fillets (about 120g each)
- 200ml Gochujang Sauce (page 185), plus extra for drizzling
- 1 lime, halved, plus wedges to serve
- 1 tbsp toasted sesame seeds (mix of black and white)
- 1 red chilli, thinly sliced (optional)
- Small handful of fresh coriander leaves, chopped

FOR THE RICE BOWL
- 600g cooked Coconut Rice (page 152)
- Smashed Cucumber Salad (page 154)
- 1 avocado, smashed with the juice of 1 lime
- Kale Miso Slaw (page 101)

### METHOD
**1.** Coat the salmon fillets in three-quarters of the gochujang sauce and leave to marinate in the fridge for at least 30 minutes (longer if you've got the time). Meanwhile, cook your coconut rice and prep the sides: the cucumber salad, smashed avo and that ridiculously moreish kale miso slaw.

**2.** Preheat the oven to 220°C fan (240°C/465°F) and line a baking tray with baking parchment. Lay the salmon fillets skin-side down on the tray and roast for 7 minutes until just cooked through and sticky on top. While the salmon's still hot, squeeze over some lime, drizzle with the remaining gochujang sauce, and get ready to build your bowl.

**3.** Start with a big spoon of warm coconut rice. Add the smashed cucumber, a scoop of avocado and a pile of kale miso slaw. Top with a glazed salmon fillet, scatter over some sesame seeds, sliced red chilli (if using) and fresh coriander. Serve with a wedge of lime and another drizzle of sauce if you're feeling saucy.

> **Tip**
> Want to go veggie or just love a bit of crispy tofu? Swap the salmon fillets for 400g firm tofu, pressed and cut into chunky cubes. Toss them in a little oil and roast at 200°C fan (220°C/425°F) for 25-30 minutes until golden and crisp at the edges. Once roasted, coat the tofu in the gochujang sauce just like the salmon. You can even chuck it back in the oven for 5-10 minutes to get that sauce nice and sticky.

# Gochujang Aubergine

Ve / DF

Sweet, sticky, spicy, silky. Here aubergine is roasted until soft and golden, then tossed in a punchy miso gochujang glaze that clings to every crevice. Potentially one of those dishes that makes a strong case for going meatless. Pile it high on rice, serve it as a side, or enjoy it as a fantastic veg main.

**SERVES 4**
**PREP TIME: 15 MINS**
**COOK TIME: 30–40 MINS**

## INGREDIENTS
- 2 large aubergines, cut into 2.5cm rounds
- 2 tbsp olive oil
- 1 tbsp toasted sesame seeds
- Handful of fresh coriander or chives, chopped
- 2 spring onions, thinly sliced
- 1 tsp chilli flakes (optional)
- Sea salt and black pepper

FOR THE MISO GOCHUJANG SAUCE
- 2 tbsp white or yellow miso
- 4 tbsp Gochujang Sauce (page 185)
- 3 tbsp mirin
- 1 tbsp soy sauce
- Juice of 1 lime

## METHOD

**1.** Preheat the oven to 200°C fan (220°C/425°F). Sprinkle your aubergine rounds with salt and let them sit for 10 minutes; this helps draw out moisture and gives a better roast. Pat dry and remove the excess salt.

**2.** Toss the aubergines with the olive oil and some black pepper and lay them out in a single layer on a parchment-lined baking tray. Roast for 25-30 minutes, flipping once, until golden and properly soft all the way through.

**3.** While the aubergines roast, mix your miso, gochujang sauce, mirin, soy sauce and lime juice in a large bowl until smooth. Taste it; it should be bold, sweet-salty and a little spicy.

**4.** Once the aubergine is ready, toss it straight in the sauce while it's still hot. Let every piece get coated and glossy. If you want it extra sticky, chuck it back in the oven for another 5-10 minutes.

**5.** Plate up the aubergine, then scatter with sesame seeds, coriander or chives, sliced spring onion and a little chilli if you want some extra heat.

# Gochujang Prawns + Rice Noodles
DF

Sticky, spicy prawns. Slurpy rice noodles. Crisp veg, fresh herbs and – just when you think it's done – bam, crushed roasted peanuts for the perfect savoury crunch. It's the kind of bowl you don't want to share.

**SERVES 4**
**PREP TIME: 20 MINS**
**COOK TIME: 15 MINS**

## INGREDIENTS
- 1 tbsp shop-bought gochujang
- 1 tbsp soy sauce
- 1 tbsp honey
- 1 garlic clove, grated
- 1 tsp toasted sesame oil
- Pinch of sea salt
- 400g raw shell-on prawns
- Splash of avocado oil
- ½ red chilli, thinly sliced (optional)
- 2 lemons, halved, to serve

FOR THE DRESSING
- 3-4 tbsp Gochujang Sauce (page 185)
- 1 tbsp lime juice
- 1 tbsp soy sauce
- 1 tsp rice vinegar
- 1 tsp maple syrup or honey
- 1 tsp toasted sesame oil

FOR THE NOODLES AND VEG
- 250g rice noodles
- 1 carrot, peeled and sliced into matchsticks
- 1 cucumber, deseeded and sliced into matchsticks
- 1 red pepper, thinly sliced
- 1 tbsp sesame seeds, toasted
- 2 spring onions, thinly sliced
- 50g crushed roasted peanuts
- Small handful of fresh coriander leaves
- Small handful of fresh mint leaves

## METHOD
**1.** Start with the prawns. Mix the gochujang, soy sauce, honey, garlic, sesame oil and salt in a bowl. Add the prawns and let them sit while you prep the noodles and veg.

**2.** Whisk together all the dressing ingredients, then taste and adjust to your liking: it should be punchy, sweet, spicy and a bit sour.

**3.** Cook the noodles according to the packet instructions, then rinse with cold water and drain well. Toss into a large bowl with the carrot, cucumber, red pepper and sesame seeds, Add most of the spring onions, the crushed roasted peanuts and herbs and most of the dressing and toss gently to combine.

**4.** Heat a heavy-based frying pan over a high heat with a splash of avocado oil. Sear the prawns for 1–2 minutes on each side until just cooked. Add the lemon wedges, cut-side down, to the hot pan and press them down for a few minutes, without moving them around, until nicely charred. Set aside. Add the lemon wedges, cut-side down, to the hot pan and press them down for a few minutes, without moving them around, until nicely charred.

**5.** Divide the noodle salad between bowls. Top with the prawns, the sliced chilli and remaining herbs and spring onion. Drizzle over the rest of the dressing and serve hot with a charred lemon half for squeezing.

### Tip
You can swap the prawns for tofu if you're going plant-based. Use firm tofu, cut into cubes, and pan-fry until golden before tossing it in the sauce.

GOCHUJANG

# Charred Corn Ribs + Gochujang Mayo

V / GF (use gluten-free gochujang)

These corn ribs are smoky, spicy, a little sweet and totally addictive. Perfect for barbecues, snacks, or just because. Gochujang mayo on the side? Non-negotiable. You'll be licking your fingers, and probably the plate.

**SERVES 4 AS A SIDE**
**PREP TIME: 15 MINS**
**COOK TIME: 20–25 MINS (OVEN) OR 7–10 MINS (GRILL/BBQ)**

### INGREDIENTS
- 4 corn cobs, husks removed
- 4 tbsp shop-bought gochujang
- ½ tbsp olive oil
- 1 tbsp lemon salt (see below)
- 1–2 tbsp gochugaru (optional)
- Black pepper
- Small handful of chopped fresh coriander (optional)

FOR THE GOCHUJANG MAYO
- 220g mayo (homemade or shop-bought)
- 115g Gochujang Sauce (page 185)
- 2 tbsp finely chopped chives

### METHOD

**1.** Preheat the oven to 200°C fan (220°C/425°F) or fire up the grill or barbecue to medium-high.

**2.** Slice each corn cob lengthways into quarters or sixths. This takes a bit of muscle – use a sharp knife and be careful.

**3.** Mix the gochujang with ½ tablespoon of the olive oil to loosen it slightly, then brush it all over the corn ribs. Get right in there, every kernel should be coated. Sprinkle over the lemon salt, a grind of black pepper and gochugaru (if you're going for heat).

**4.** Roast in the oven for 20-25 minutes, flipping halfway, or grill or barbecue for 7-10 minutes, turning regularly until charred and tender.

**5.** While the corn is cooking, stir together the mayo and gochujang sauce until smooth. Fold in the chopped chives. Try not to eat it all with a spoon.

**6.** Once the corn's done, pile it on to a plate, drizzle (or dollop) over the gochujang mayo, and scatter over the chopped coriander (if using).

HOW TO MAKE LEMON SALT

Finely grate the zest of 1 unwaxed lemon, avoiding the white pith, then spread out on a plate and leave it out in the sun or a warm, dry spot for a few hours until fully dry. Alternatively, dry it in a low oven (around 80°C) for 30-40 minutes. You should end up with about 1 tablespoon of dried lemon zest. Mix this with ½ teaspoon of sea salt and ¼ teaspoon of black pepper.

# PULSES, *Grains* & Wheat

| **Freekeh** | **Chickpeas** | **Dried Pasta** | **Flour + Bread** |
| *196* | *204* | *214* | *230* |

# Freekeh

*the grain we've had since day one*

---

Let's talk about freekeh. It's been on the menu at Farmer J since day one, and there's a reason for that. It's nutty, chewy and actually has flavour (not many grains do). We love it because it brings real depth to a dish – it's slightly smoky, savoury and far more interesting than your usual rice or quinoa. It's hearty without being heavy. It's what you reach for when you want the base of your bowl to do more than just show up. It's there to deliver.

Some facts for you: freekeh is wheat that is harvested when young, roasted over an open flame, then rubbed to remove the husk. That's right, picked while it's still green, then fire-smoked. And if you like a bit of backstory with your lunch, freekeh's got it in spades. This stuff goes back thousands of years, all the way to the Fertile Crescent, the cradle of farming itself. It even gets a name drop in the Bible (not that I am a regular reader). It was born out of survival: smoking this early harvest of green wheat preserved it so it could be stored to get people through the leaner times. So just remember, when you cook with freekeh, you're not just making lunch, you're keeping a seriously good ancient habit alive.

# Farmer's Grains

Ve / DF

This is how we've served freekeh since day one. It's the bedrock of your Fieldtray, the perfect grainy base for harissa chicken, spicy green tahini, or whatever else you've got going. Freekeh brings the chew, bulgur brings the comfort, and crispy onions bring the joy. We bake it all together in one tray because life's too short for faffy pans. Serve warm and don't skip the fork fluff.

**SERVES 6–8**
**PREP TIME: 5 MINS**
**COOK TIME: 25 MINS**

## INGREDIENTS

- 500g freekeh
- 500g coarse bulgur wheat
- 100g crispy onions (or caramelised onions)
- 1½ tbsp za'atar spice blend
- 1 tsp sea salt
- 1 tsp ground cumin
- 1 tsp ground cinnamon (optional)
- 1.5 litres lukewarm water
- Chopped fresh parsley, to serve

## METHOD

**1.** Preheat the oven to 200°C fan (220°C/425°F). Into a large baking dish or deep roasting tray, chuck the freekeh, bulgur, crispy onions, za'atar, salt and whatever spices you're using. Give it all a quick stir. Pour over the lukewarm water and stir gently to combine. Cover the tray tightly with foil (or a lid if it fits). Roast in the oven for 20-25 minutes until all the water's absorbed and the grains are tender but still have a nice bite.

**2.** Fluff the grains with a fork, and finish with a generous handful of chopped parsley. Serve warm, preferably under a mound of harissa chicken and spicy green tahini.

# Freekeh Tabouleh + Roasted Cauliflower

V

Tabouleh but heartier. We've swapped bulgur for nutty freekeh, thrown in crispy roasted cauliflower, and finished the whole lot with creamy feta. A proper salad-salad. Fresh herbs, sharp pickled onions, a lemony kick and just enough cumin to keep things interesting. It works warm or cold, as a side or a meal.

**SERVES 4 AS A SIDE OR 2 AS A MAIN**
**PREP TIME: 15 MINS (PLUS SOAKING)**
**COOK TIME: 15–20 MINS**

### INGREDIENTS
- 100g freekeh
- ½ head of cauliflower (about 350g), roughly chopped
- 2 tbsp olive oil
- ½ tsp coriander seeds, lightly crushed with your fingers
- 1–2 celery sticks, diced
- 2 tbsp Quick Pickled Red Onion (page 161)
- Handful of fresh parsley, chopped
- Handful of fresh mint, chopped
- Handful of fresh coriander, chopped
- Juice of ½ lemon
- ½ tsp ground cumin
- 100g feta cheese, crumbled
- Handful of sliced almonds, toasted
- Sea salt and black pepper

### METHOD
**1.** Preheat the oven to 200°C fan (220°C/425°F) and boil a full kettle of water.

**2.** Start by rinsing the freekeh under cold water. Then soak it in the just-boiled water for 30 minutes while you get on with everything else.

**3.** Toss the roughly chopped cauliflower and its leaves with 1 tablespoon of the olive oil and a good pinch of salt. Add the crushed coriander seeds and toss again to coat. Spread out on a baking tray and roast for 15–20 minutes, flipping halfway, until golden and crisp at the edges.

**4.** Drain the soaked freekeh well, then add to a large bowl with the celery, pickled red onion and roughly chopped fresh herbs. Add the roasted cauliflower and its crispy leaves and toss gently to combine.

**5.** Whisk the remaining tablespoon of olive oil with the lemon juice, cumin and a grind of black pepper. Taste and adjust the seasoning, then drizzle over the salad and mix well.

**6.** Crumble the feta over the top and finish with toasted almonds. Serve straight away or chill for 30 minutes to let the flavours come together – it only gets better.

FREEKEH

# Stuffed Onions + Tahini Sauce

Ve / DF

If you've never stuffed an onion before, now's the time. This dish is sweet, savoury, earthy, nutty and properly comforting. The freekeh and lentils soak up all that spiced stock, the onions go soft and sweet in the oven, and the tahini cuts right through with richness and bite. It's a bit involved, but it's worth it. One of our favourites.

**SERVES 4**
**PREP TIME: 40 MINS**
**COOK TIME: 2 HOURS**

### INGREDIENTS
- 4 tbsp olive oil
- 5 medium white onions, 1 thinly sliced (leave the others whole for now)
- 180g freekeh
- 190g beluga lentils, soaked overnight and drained
- 1 tsp ground cumin
- 720ml water
- 2 tomatoes, sliced
- A few sprigs of thyme
- 1 litre vegetable stock or water
- 100g date molasses
- Sea salt and black pepper
- Chopped fresh parsley or coriander, to serve

FOR THE TAHINI SAUCE
- 120g tahini
- 120ml water (ideally ice-cold)
- 60ml olive oil
- 2 garlic cloves, grated
- 60ml lemon juice
- 2 tsp lemon zest

### METHOD

**1.** Heat the olive oil in a large saucepan and cook the sliced onion over a low heat for 15-20 minutes, or until soft and golden. Stir in the freekeh, lentils and cumin and season with salt and pepper. Add the water and bring to the boil, then reduce the heat and simmer with the lid on for 30-40 minutes until the grains are cooked through and all the water has been absorbed. Let it sit off the heat for 10 minutes to steam and fluff up.

**2.** Meanwhile, prep your onions. Peel off the outer layer of skin, but keep the root end intact. Cut a slit vertically, just halfway through. Bring a pan of salted water to the boil, add the onions and cook for 10-15 minutes until soft, then drain and leave to cool.

**3.** Preheat the oven to 160°C fan (180°C/350°F).

**4.** Gently peel away the onion layers. Spoon the freekeh-lentil mix on to each layer and fold into snug little parcels.

**5.** Line a roasting tray with any leftover onion bits. Arrange your stuffed onions in the tray and tuck in the tomato slices and thyme. Mix the veg stock with the date molasses and pour this around the onions. Season with black pepper, cover tightly with foil and bake for 1½ hours until the onions are tender and golden.

**6.** While they're in the oven, make the tahini sauce. Blend together all the sauce ingredients with a pinch of sea salt until smooth and pourable.

**7.** To serve, spoon the tahini sauce on to a big platter. Pile the stuffed onions on top and finish with a handful of herbs.

# Tommy's Freekancini

This one's from Tom, our Head of Quality, food obsessive and all-round outstanding chef. These freekeh arancini are his genius take on the Italian classic – golden, crunchy, cheesy, herby bites made with nutty freekeh and stuffed with feta and Parmesan. Perfect for a party, or just because. They fly off the tray every time.
(Image on page 78, topped with Spicy Green Tahini and chives)

**MAKES ABOUT 15–18 ARANCINI**
**PREP TIME: 30 MINS (PLUS COOLING AND CHILLING)**
**COOK TIME: 45 MINS**

### INGREDIENTS
- 4 tbsp olive oil
- 2 shallots, finely diced
- 2 sprigs of fresh oregano or thyme, leaves picked
- 200g freekeh
- 950ml boiling water or veg stock
- 100g feta cheese, crumbled
- 100g Parmesan, grated
- Zest of ½ lemon
- Plain flour, sifted
- 2–3 eggs, well beaten
- Breadcrumbs or panko
- Neutral oil for deep-frying
- Sea salt and black pepper

### METHOD

**1.** Heat the olive oil in a wide frying pan over a medium heat. Add the shallots and cook for 6–7 minutes until soft and golden. Add the oregano or thyme and stir for another minute, then add the freekeh, season with salt and pepper and stir well. Toast for 2–3 minutes until the grains are all coated. Gradually add the boiling water or stock, stirring in about a cup of the liquid at a time before adding more (as if you were making a risotto). Taste and adjust the seasoning, then simmer over a low heat for 20–25 minutes until the grains are cooked through, adding a splash more water if needed. Cool the cooked risotto on a tray, then chill in the fridge for at least 2 hours.

**2.** Once cold, mix in the feta, Parmesan and lemon zest. Taste and season again if needed. Wet your hands slightly and roll the mixture into balls, about 3–4cm wide. Place on a tray and chill again.

**3.** Set up three shallow dishes: one with flour, one with beaten eggs, one with breadcrumbs. Roll each ball in flour, then egg, then breadcrumbs. Tip: use one hand for wet, one for dry to avoid a claggy mess.

**4.** Chill the coated arancini while you heat the oil in a deep frying pan to 170–180°C. If you don't have a thermometer, drop in a pinch of breadcrumbs – they should sizzle immediately but not burn.

**5.** Fry the arancini in batches for 4–5 minutes until golden and crispy. Remove and drain on kitchen paper. These are best eaten 5 minutes after frying, while the centre is warm and gooey, so keep warm in a low oven if needed.

**6.** Serve with any dip you like – pesto, aioli, yoghurt, or good old ketchup.

# Mushroom + Freekeh Risotto + Skordalia

Ve / DF

This one sounds a bit cheffy, but it is everything we love about food: rich, earthy, deeply savoury and comforting without being heavy. A favourite of Nitai's to cook, and one of mine to eat. We use freekeh instead of rice for its nutty bite, build layers of flavour with mushrooms and finish with a velvety almond skordalia that makes it feel decadent, even though it's vegan.

**SERVES 2**
**PREP TIME: 15 MINS**
**COOK TIME: 1 HOUR**

## INGREDIENTS

FOR THE SKORDALIA (CELERIAC-ALMOND CREAM)
- 200g celeriac, peeled and roughly chopped
- 1 garlic clove, grated
- 50g blanched almonds
- ½ tbsp olive oil
- ½ tbsp lemon juice
- Water or vegetable stock, to loosen
- Sea salt and black pepper

FOR THE ROASTED MUSHROOMS
- 100g oyster mushrooms, sliced (or other mushrooms if you can't source these)
- 1 tbsp olive oil

FOR THE RISOTTO
- ½ tbsp olive oil
- 1 shallot, finely chopped
- 1 garlic clove, grated
- 100g mixed mushrooms (cremini, shiitake, button), roughly torn if large
- 100g freekeh
- 500ml hot vegetable stock
- ½ tsp fresh thyme leaves or ¼ tsp dried thyme
- ½ tbsp lemon juice
- Chopped fresh parsley or chives, to serve

## METHOD

**1.** Get the skordalia going first. Add the chopped celeriac to a pan of salted water, bring to the boil and cook for 15–20 minutes until fork-tender. Drain well, then chuck it into a blender with the garlic, almonds, olive oil, lemon juice and a good pinch of salt and pepper. Blitz until smooth and creamy, adding a splash of water or veg stock to loosen. Keep it warm – this will be your flavour bomb and vegan butter in the risotto.

**2.** You can make the roasted mushrooms, while the celeriac is simmering. Preheat the oven to 200°C fan (220°C/425°F). Toss the oyster mushrooms in olive oil, season well and roast for 10–15 minutes until golden and crispy. Set aside while you make the risotto.

**3.** Heat the olive oil in a large pan over a low-medium heat, then sauté the shallot for 5 minutes until soft. Add the garlic and mixed mushrooms and cook for another 5 minutes until the mushrooms start to give up their liquid. Stir in the freekeh and let it toast for 2 minutes. Then slowly start adding the hot veg stock a ladle at a time, letting the freekeh absorb it before adding more. After each ladleful, stir in a tablespoon or two of skordalia. Keep going like that, stirring often, for 25–30 minutes, until the freekeh is cooked with a little chew left. Once the risotto is creamy and cooked, stir through the thyme and lemon juice. Taste and season.

**4.** Spoon into bowls, top with the crispy oyster mushrooms, and finish with a swirl of olive oil or a little more skordalia and a sprinkle of fresh herbs.

# Chickpeas

*I'm allergic, but you should eat them*

---

This is actually quite a painful chapter for me to write. Emotionally *and* physically. I found out about a year ago that I'm allergic to chickpeas. No joke, this is true. For a while I thought it was sesame (cue panic over tahini), but turned out it was chickpeas. Not *quite* as devastating but still pretty terrible. So yes, I can no longer eat hummus. Let that sink in. No hummus. No falafel. No crispy chickpeas in salads. Nothing. Anyway, enough about me.

If *you're* not allergic, you must try these recipes. At Farmer J, chickpeas are one of our most-used ingredients; roasted until crisp, you'll find them tossed through a salad every season.

Hummus alone deserves its own fan club. It's rich, savoury, moreish and just happens to go with everything, from pickles and eggs to roasted veg and grilled meat. And beyond hummus, chickpeas are total workhorses: they carry spice beautifully, hold their shape when roasted, and give texture and heart to whatever they're thrown into.

# Quickie Hummus, Za'atar Aubergine + Soft-boiled Egg

V / GF / DF

We're not here to start a hummus fight. We'll save that for the next book. But if you need a quick, creamy fix to get you through the week, this one's solid. Pro tip: use decent chickpeas (the big jarred ones are great) and a splash of ice-cold water, which helps create the smoothness. Topped with roasted aubergine and jammy eggs, this makes a brilliant brunch.

**SERVES 4**
**PREP TIME: 15 MINS**
**COOK TIME: 20 MINS**

### INGREDIENTS
- 2 x 400g tins good-quality chickpeas (or use the big, creamy jarred ones if you can find them)
- 100g tahini
- Juice of ½ lemon
- Pinch of sea salt
- Pinch of ground cumin
- 50–75ml chickpea liquid or ice-cold water (more if needed)

FOR THE AUBERGINE AND EGGS
- 1 aubergine, sliced into 2cm rounds (or lengthways into thin wedges)
- 4 tbsp olive oil, plus extra for drizzling
- 2 tbsp za'atar spice blend, plus a pinch to serve
- 2 eggs
- 1 tbsp sesame seeds, to serve

### METHOD

**1.** Warm one tin of chickpeas in their liquid for a few minutes to loosen them up. Drain (reserving the liquid) and blend with the tahini, lemon juice, salt and cumin. Add a splash of cold water or chickpea liquid as you blend to get it smooth and creamy. Taste and adjust the salt or lemon. Keep warm or at room temperature – it's good either way.

**2.** Preheat the oven to 200°C fan (220°C/425°F). Toss the aubergine slices with olive oil and za'atar, lay them out on a baking tray and roast for 8–10 minutes until soft and golden on the edges.

**3.** Meanwhile, bring a pan of water to the boil, lower in the eggs and boil for 7 minutes, then plunge them into ice-cold water to stop the cooking. Peel and halve – you should have just-set jammy yolks.

**4.** Drain and rinse the remaining tin of chickpeas. Spoon the hummus on to a big plate. Top with the drained chickpeas, roasted aubergine and halved eggs. Finish with a drizzle of olive oil, a sprinkle of sesame seeds and an extra pinch of za'atar.

CHICKPEAS

# Green Chickpea Masabacha

Ve / GF / DF

I can hear you asking, what the heck is a green chickpea? They are basically unripe, young chickpeas, harvested early. Green chickpeas are fresh, nutty and a bit grassy – a totally different vibe from their beige, tinned cousins. Now masabacha, what's that? It is hummus's looser, chunkier sibling, and we love it. Here, warm chickpeas get coated in lemony tahini and spooned over a creamy swipe of tahini. Good olive oil and a hit of lemon zest take it to another level. Serve it with pitta or flatbread.

**SERVES 2–3**
**PREP TIME: 10 MINS**
**COOK TIME: 5 MINS**

### INGREDIENTS
- 300g cooked green chickpeas (see Note)
- 25g raw tahini
- ½ garlic clove, crushed
- Zest of 1 lemon, plus extra to serve
- Juice of ½ lemon (about 1 tbsp)
- 1 tsp ground cumin
- 150g Classic Tahini Sauce (page 83)
- Good-quality olive oil, for drizzling
- Sea salt and black pepper

### METHOD

**1.** Warm the chickpeas gently in a small pan with a splash of water over a low heat, just enough to take the chill off. Don't cook them into mush; they should still hold a bit of bite.

**2.** While they're warming, mix the raw tahini, garlic, lemon zest and juice, cumin, salt and loads of black pepper in a small bowl. Stir until smooth. If it seizes up (it probably will!), add splashes of cold water and stir until you get a loose, silky texture.

**3.** In another bowl or small plate, spread the classic tahini sauce in a wide swoop. This is your creamy base.

**4.** Toss the warm chickpeas in the tahini dressing, then spoon them generously over the tahini base. Drizzle with olive oil and top with extra lemon zest. Serve warm with hot pitta or fresh flatbread and scoop away.

### Note
Can't find green chickpeas (sometimes called green chana)? Try an Indian or Middle Eastern shop, or look in the freezer section. If not, no stress. Use regular chickpeas instead (just make sure they're decent quality). The tahini and lemon will still carry the dish beautifully.

CHICKPEAS

207

# Roasted Aubergine, Hispi Cabbage + Za'atar Chickpeas + Spicy Aubergine Tahini

Ve / GF / DF

This is one of those plant-based bangers that eats like a main. Charred cabbage, caramelised aubergine, crispy chickpeas, all tied together with a spicy aubergine tahini so good you'll want to put it on everything. A proper showcase of chickpeas done right. No meat, no dairy, no problem.

**SERVES 4**
**PREP TIME: 15 MINS**
**COOK TIME: 1 HOUR**

### INGREDIENTS

FOR THE ROASTED AUBERGINE
- 2 medium aubergines, sliced into rounds
- 3–4 tbsp olive oil
- 1 tbsp za'atar spice blend
- Sea salt and black pepper

FOR THE ROASTED HISPI AND CHICKPEAS
- 1 hispi cabbage (600–700g), cut into 8 wedges
- 3 tbsp olive oil
- 2 tbsp za'atar spice blend
- 400g tin chickpeas, drained and rinsed
- 1 tsp sumac

FOR THE SPICY AUBERGINE TAHINI
- 1 small aubergine
- 100g tahini
- 50g pickled green chillies, roughly chopped (use milder chillies or less if you don't like too much heat)
- 2½ tbsp pickled chilli liquid
- 1–2 tsp sea salt
- 30g fresh parsley, chopped
- Juice of ½ large lemon
- 1 tsp ground cumin
- 50ml olive oil

TO SERVE
- Small handful of fresh parsley, chopped
- Sliced green chilli (optional)
- A sprinkle of sumac

## METHOD

**1.** Preheat the oven to 200°C fan (220°C/425°F) and line a roasting tray with baking parchment.

**2.** Start with the aubergine. Toss the slices with the olive oil, za'atar and some salt and pepper, then roast on the lined tray for 25-30 minutes, flipping halfway, until golden and soft.

**3.** While that's going, get the cabbage wedges on to a separate roasting tray. Toss them with 2 tablespoons of the olive oil, a tablespoon of the za'atar and some salt and pepper, then do the same with the chickpeas, tossing them with the remaining olive oil and za'atar and the sumac. Season with salt and pepper. Spread out on the tray next to the cabbage wedges and roast for 10-15 minutes until the cabbage is crisp but the inside's still got some bite and the chickpeas are just crispy.

**4.** Now the good stuff: the sauce. Roast the aubergine at 220°C fan (240°C/465°F) for 35-40 minutes, until properly soft and collapsed. Scoop out the flesh and blitz it smooth in a blender or food processor. Add the tahini, pickled chillies, pickle liquid, salt, parsley, lemon juice, cumin and olive oil. Blend until creamy, gradually adding a tablespoon or two of ice-cold water to loosen. Taste and adjust the seasoning with more salt or lemon.

**5.** To assemble, arrange the roasted aubergine, hispi cabbage and crispy chickpeas in an ovenproof serving dish, then whack it back in the oven for 5 minutes to bring it all together.

**6.** Serve with a generous drizzle of the aubergine tahini, chopped parsley, sliced green chillies if you like heat, and a sprinkle of sumac. Serve warm.

# Chickpea Fish Stew

GF / DF

A rich, spicy chickpea stew that's perfect for dunking fresh bread into, with fish gently poached right on top. We call it a stew, but it's light enough for lunch, or even brunch. Packed with flavour, boosted with harissa and finished with fresh coriander and preserved lemon for lift.

**SERVES 4**
**PREP TIME: 20 MINS**
**COOK TIME: 45–50 MINS**

### INGREDIENTS

- 2–3 tbsp olive oil, plus extra for drizzling
- 2 tbsp harissa paste
- 3 garlic cloves, crushed
- 1 tbsp sweet paprika
- 1 tsp coriander seeds
- 1 tsp cumin seeds
- 2 red or yellow peppers, cut into 2–3cm chunks
- 1 tbsp tomato purée
- 400g tin good-quality chopped tomatoes (we like San Marzano)
- 240ml lukewarm water
- 400g tin or jar chickpeas, drained and rinsed
- 4 skinless fish fillets (such as bass, bream, tuna or salmon), 120–150g each
- Small handful of fresh coriander, chopped
- 1 tbsp Preserved Lemon (page 175), finely chopped
- Sea salt and black pepper

TO SERVE
- Warm flatbread or rice
- Spicy Green Tahini (page 83)

### METHOD

**1.** Heat the olive oil in a large pan or casserole over a medium heat, then add the harissa. Let it cook out for 3–4 minutes to deepen in flavour. Add the garlic and stir until just soft, then throw in the paprika and coriander and cumin seeds. Give everything a quick stir and let it bloom for 1–2 minutes.

**2.** Add the peppers and cook for 8–10 minutes until softened and slightly golden at the edges before adding the tomato purée and chopped tomatoes. Season with a teaspoon of salt and some pepper, pour in the lukewarm water and bring to a gentle simmer. Let it bubble away gently for about 20 minutes, half-covered, stirring occasionally. Once the base is looking rich and thick, stir in the chickpeas. Let that simmer for another 20 minutes to soak up all that spice and tomato goodness.

**3.** Meanwhile, season the fish fillets with sea salt and let them sit for 5–10 minutes. Rinse under cold water and pat dry. When the stew is ready, stir in half the coriander. Gently lay the fish fillets on top, skin-side up if using skin-on. Scatter over the remaining coriander and the preserved lemon, then drizzle a little olive oil over the top. Pop the lid on and let it cook gently for about 12–15 minutes, just until the fish is cooked through and flakes easily. No overcooking please.

**4.** Taste for seasoning one last time. Serve hot, with warm flatbread or rice and a dollop of spicy green tahini if you've got it.

### Tip

Use a firm fish like sea bass or tuna for best results (salmon works too, it's just softer), and go easy on the harissa — it should warm you up, not blow your head off.

CHICKPEAS

# Chickpea Crumble + Cavolo Nero Salad
GF

When Nitai first made this, we fell in love with it instantly. Crunchy, savoury, creamy – just a banger of a salad. It's great on its own or next to grilled meat or fish.

**SERVES 2 AS A MAIN OR 4 AS A SIDE**
**PREP TIME: 15 MINS**
**COOK TIME: 20 MINS**

### INGREDIENTS
- 400g tin chickpeas, drained and rinsed
- 4 tbsp olive oil
- 1 tsp sumac
- 1 tsp ground cumin
- 200g cavolo nero, stalks removed, leaves torn into bite-sized pieces
- Sea salt and black pepper
- Quick Pickled Red Onions (page 161), to finish

### FOR THE TAHINI CAESAR DRESSING
- 40g tahini
- 2 tbsp lemon juice
- 1 garlic clove, grated
- 90ml olive oil
- 40g finely grated Parmesan, plus extra to serve

### METHOD
**1.** Preheat the oven to 160°C fan (180°C/350°F). Pat the chickpeas dry with a clean towel – this helps them crisp up properly – then toss with 2 tablespoons of the olive oil, the sumac, cumin and a pinch of salt. Spread out on a baking tray and roast for 15-18 minutes, shaking halfway, until golden and just starting to crisp. You don't want them rock hard, just crumbly. Let them cool slightly, then crush gently with the back of a spoon. You're aiming for a mix of chunks and small bits.

**2.** On another tray, toss the cavolo nero with the remaining 2 tablespoons of olive oil and some salt and pepper. Roast for 15 minutes alongside the chickpeas until crisp around the edges but still green.

**3.** Meanwhile, make the dressing. Whisk the tahini, lemon juice, garlic and a pinch of salt and pepper until smooth. Slowly drizzle in the olive oil while whisking continuously until emulsified. Stir in the Parmesan. If it's too thick, loosen with a little cold water or more lemon juice, then taste and adjust the seasoning.

**4.** To assemble the salad, spread the crispy cavolo nero on to a serving plate. Scatter over the crushed chickpeas, then spoon over the dressing. Layer on the pickled onions, then hit it again with more dressing. Finish with another grating of Parmesan and a good grind of black pepper.

### Tip
Serve this one straight away, while the chickpeas are still warm and crumbly and the cavolo's nice and crisp. Don't let it sit. Great with pitta, grilled chicken, or just on its own with a cold drink.

CHICKPEAS

# Dried Pasta

*the backbone of the pantry*

---

Dried pasta. Not exactly a head-turner of a name, is it? Sounds a bit plain, a bit pantry-basic. But let's be honest, *proper* pasta is pure joy. It's comfort and chaos in a bowl. A blank canvas for whatever's knocking about in your fridge or cupboard. A pantry hero if ever there was one. And while fresh pasta gets all the glossy cookbook love, dried pasta is the real backbone. Affordable, reliable, and always ready for action. You want dinner in under 20 minutes? Dried pasta's your mate.

At Farmer J, our love story with pasta is mostly about the mac'. Our mac and cheese is the most-ordered side on the menu for a reason. It's creamy, salty, gooey, has a slight hit of chilli and we change up the veg with the seasons, so it's kind of healthy too. Kale and broccoli, squash to shroom and truffle. You could throw it next to anything, chicken, steak, or just a big pile of pickles and it'll hold its own. We've seen people order it as a main with *another* serving as a side. Respect.

At home, it's a full-blown obsession. Jonathan's a pasta genius, rigorous about flavour and seasoning, and never afraid of adding anchovies. Nitai, on the other hand, is married to an Italian, which means pasta is practically religion.

In this section we are not just thinking carbonara and cacio e pepe: Farmer J pasta is pantry-led, hearty, bold, and never too neat.

# Bucatini al Forno + Bolognese Ragù

This is the pasta bake to end all pasta bakes. Think bolognese meets lasagne, minus the faff. Bucatini gets tossed through a rich, slow-cooked beef ragù, layered with creamy béchamel, mozzarella and Parmesan, then baked until golden and bubbling. Serve in fat slabs or crispy-edged cubes. It's weekend cooking at its absolute finest.
(Image on page 248)

**SERVES 4–6**
**PREP TIME: 25 MINS**
**COOK TIME: 1 HOUR 15 MINS**

### INGREDIENTS
FOR THE RAGÙ
- 2 tbsp olive oil
- 1 onion, finely chopped
- ½ carrot, finely chopped
- ½ celery stick, finely chopped
- 2 garlic cloves, grated
- 500g beef mince (at least 20% fat)
- 1 tbsp tomato purée
- 125ml white wine
- 125ml milk
- 400g tomato passata
- 5 drops of Worcestershire sauce
- 3 drops of Tabasco
- Sea salt and black pepper

FOR THE BÉCHAMEL
- 2 tbsp butter
- 2 tbsp plain flour
- 375ml milk
- Pinch of grated nutmeg

TO ASSEMBLE
- 400g bucatini
- Olive oil
- 200g mozzarella, grated
- 100g Parmesan, grated
- Fresh basil (optional)

### METHOD

**1.** Start with the ragù. Heat the olive oil in a large pan and add the onion, carrot and celery. Cook over a medium heat for 5–7 minutes until soft. Add the garlic, cook for 1 minute more, then tip in the beef. Brown it all over, breaking it up with a wooden spoon.

**2.** Stir in the tomato purée, season well and pour in the white wine. Let it bubble for a couple of minutes to cook off the booze. Add the milk and simmer to reduce to a couple of tablespoons, then stir in the passata. Simmer over a low heat for 45–60 minutes, stirring now and then. Finish with the Worcestershire and Tabasco.

**3.** While that's going, make the béchamel. Melt the butter in a pan, stir in the flour and cook for 1–2 minutes. Slowly whisk in the milk until smooth. Cook for 5–7 minutes until thickened. Season and add a pinch of nutmeg, then set aside.

**4.** Preheat the oven to 160°C fan (180°C/350°F).

**5.** Cook the bucatini in a large pan of salted boiling water until al dente. Drain and toss with a little olive oil to stop it sticking.

**6.** Mix the cooked bucatini with the ragù in a large ovenproof dish. Stir in half the mozzarella, half the Parmesan and the béchamel. Stir well. Top with the rest of the cheeses and bake for 20–25 minutes until golden and bubbling. Let it rest for a few minutes before cutting into slabs.

**7.** Optional finishing move: chill it, then pan-sear or re-bake the squares for crispy edges. Tear over some basil leaves to serve (if liked).

DRIED PASTA

# Sausage, Porcini + Fennel Pasta

This has all the flavour of a slow-cooked ragù but without the faff. This is Jonathan's pasta; just like the mac is Ali's, it's his signature dish. It's rich, earthy, lemony and packed with flavour. We're not trying to be delicate here; it's big, bold and properly satisfying.

**SERVES 4**
**PREP TIME: 10 MINS**
**COOK TIME: 30–35 MINS**

## INGREDIENTS
- 20g dried porcini mushrooms
- 300ml chicken stock
- 2 tbsp olive oil, plus more if needed
- 300g fennel sausages (or use plain sausages and 1 tsp fennel seeds)
- 2 garlic cloves, finely chopped
- 1 fennel bulb, halved and thinly sliced
- 2 portobello mushrooms, roughly chopped into 2–3cm chunks
- 100ml white wine
- 1 tsp anchovy paste or 1 anchovy, finely chopped
- A few sprigs of thyme
- ½ tsp dried chilli flakes (or more, if you like it spicy)
- Zest of 1 lemon and the juice of ½, plus wedges for serving
- 350g linguine, pappardelle or tagliatelle
- 50g Parmesan, shaved or grated, to serve
- Handful of chopped flat-leaf parsley or chives
- Sea salt and black pepper

## METHOD

**1.** Start by making your porcini stock. Add the dried porcini to a pan with the chicken stock and gently warm it – no need to boil. Just let it infuse while you get going with the rest.

**2.** In a large pan, heat 1 tablespoon of the olive oil over a medium-high heat. Squeeze the sausage meat out of the casings and add to the pan, breaking it up with a wooden spoon. Cook until browned, a little crispy and just cooked through, then remove from the pan and set aside.

**3.** Add the remaining olive oil to the pan, reduce the heat a little and chuck in the garlic and sliced fennel. Cook over a medium-low heat for about 7–8 minutes, until softened. Turn up the heat, throw the sausage back in and add the portobello mushrooms. Pour in the white wine and a ladleful of the warm porcini stock. Season with salt and pepper.

**4.** Squeeze in the anchovy paste or chopped anchovy, add the thyme and chilli flakes and let the whole thing gently cook down for 10–15 minutes. Keep the stock nearby in case it needs loosening.

**5.** While that's happening, bring a large pan of salted water to the boil and cook the pasta until al dente. Drain, reserving half a mug of the pasta water.

**6.** Back to the sauce: add a splash of the reserved pasta water and the lemon zest and juice. Remove the thyme sprigs and stir through the cooked pasta until it's glossy and coated in all that good stuff.

**7.** Finish with the chopped parsley and shaved Parmesan. Give it a final grind of pepper and serve with lemon wedges on the side.

DRIED PASTA

# Farmer J Mac

V (if using vegetarian Parmesan-style cheese)

A good mac and cheese is hard to beat. And at Farmer J, this one flies out faster than we can grate the Cheddar. It's the side that people come back for, tell their mates about, and try to recreate at home. The trick? A proper béchamel, three kinds of cheese, a whisper of chilli, loads of black pepper and seasonal veg that change throughout the year.
(Image overleaf)

**SERVES 4**
**PREP TIME: 15 MINS**
**COOK TIME: 30 MINS**

### INGREDIENTS

- 400–500g seasonal veg (see facing page)
- Olive oil, for drizzling
- 450g elbow macaroni or cavatappi
- 2 tbsp unsalted butter
- 2 tbsp plain flour
- 1 litre whole milk, warmed
- 100g extra mature Cheddar, grated
- 50g Parmesan, finely grated
- Pinch of grated nutmeg (optional)
- Pinch of chilli flakes (optional)
- 100g mozzarella, grated
- Sea salt and black pepper

### METHOD

**1.** Preheat the oven to 180°C fan (200°C/400°F).

**2.** Get your veg going. Chop whatever's in season and give it a good toss with olive oil, salt and pepper. Roast until golden and soft around the edges. Set aside.

**3.** Cook the pasta in a large pan of salted boiling water until al dente. Drain and set aside.

**4.** Make the béchamel. Melt the butter in a large pan, then add the flour and whisk for 2–3 minutes until smooth. Slowly pour in the warm milk, whisking all the time to dodge lumps. Keep going until it thickens to a silky sauce. Simmer gently for a couple of minutes, then stir in the Cheddar and Parmesan until melted. Season with salt and black pepper and nutmeg and chilli flakes (if you're using them).

**5.** Add the cooked pasta and roasted veg to the cheese sauce. Stir everything together until properly coated and glorious. Tip into an ovenproof dish and top with the mozzarella. Bake for 8–10 minutes until golden, bubbling and impossible to ignore.

### Tip

For Ali's kid-friendly mac and cheese, double the Parmesan, swap out the Cheddar for 150g Gruyère, 50g mozzarella and (this is crucial) 250g mascarpone. Top the baking dish with extra Parmesan and a few handfuls of breadcrumbs, and prepare for the creamiest mac and cheese of your life.

## Seasonal veg suggestions

| SPRING | SUMMER | AUTUMN | WINTER |
|---|---|---|---|
| **Kale and broccoli** we don't waste a bit of it. Stems get grated, florets chopped, all of it roasted or blanched. | **Roasted cherry tomatoes** tossed with olive oil and thyme until jammy. | **Roasted butternut squash and sage** soft, sweet and earthy, with crispy sage for good measure. | **Mushrooms and truffle paste** rich, earthy, straight-up indulgent. |
| **Leeks and peas** sweet, soft and green. Feels like spring in a bowl. Roast the chopped leeks. Add the peas to the pasta for the last 4 minutes. | **Roasted peppers and kalamata olives** smoky, briny, sunshine-in-a-bite. | **Raw grated butternut and blue cheese** bit more punchy. You've been warned. | **Roasted Brussels sprouts** sliced thin, roasted till golden and nutty. |
| **Asparagus** some just-tender spears, roasted for about 8 minutes, do the job. | **Sweetcorn and chilli** sweet and fiery, just how we like it. | | |
| **CHEESE SHOUT** **Gruyère** nutty, melty, slightly sweet. Works like a charm with all that green. | **CHEESE SHOUT** **Feta** that salty, creamy hit stands up to all the bold summer flavours. | **CHEESE SHOUT** **Fontina** smooth and melty, the autumn jumper of cheeses. | **CHEESE SHOUT** **Parmesan and taleggio** one for tang, one for funk. Together? Magic. |

**DRIED PASTA**

# Braised Short Rib Ragù + Rigatoni

This one's from Nitai. He starts cooking it on a Sunday morning, slow and steady, and by lunchtime you've got yourself something proper special. The kind of dish that fills the house with a smell that makes people start hovering in the kitchen. It's deeply savoury, gently sweet and melts in the mouth and if you haven't had a Genovese-style ragù before, prepare to fall in love. This isn't your classic tomato-based sauce, it's all about onions, beef and slow-braising. Big pasta, big flavours.

**SERVES 4**
**PREP TIME: 25 MINS**
**COOK TIME: 3–3½ HOURS**

### INGREDIENTS
- 4 small or 2–3 large bone-in beef short ribs (about 1kg)
- 2 tbsp olive oil
- 4 large onions, thinly sliced
- 2 carrots, roughly diced
- 2 celery sticks, roughly diced
- 4 garlic cloves, crushed
- 1 tbsp tomato purée
- 2 tsp ground cumin
- 235ml white wine
- 1 tbsp date molasses
- 475ml beef stock, plus extra if needed
- 2–3 bay leaves
- Sea salt and black pepper

TO SERVE
- 350g rigatoni
- Handful of fresh parsley or basil, chopped
- Grated Parmesan (optional)

### METHOD

**1.** Preheat the oven to 140°C fan (160°C/320°F). Season the short ribs generously with salt and pepper. Heat the olive oil in a heavy-based pan or cast-iron casserole over a medium-high heat, then sear the ribs on all sides in batches until deep golden. This should take 6–7 minutes – don't be afraid to get a good colour on them. Remove from the pan and set aside.

**2.** Reduce the heat to low and tip in the sliced onions. Cook them for 15–20 minutes until they're soft, caramelised and sticky – this is where the magic starts. Add the carrots and celery, cook for another 5–8 minutes, then stir in the garlic for a minute or two more. Add the tomato purée and cumin, let it cook out for 2–3 minutes, then pour in the wine. Scrape up any bits from the bottom of the pan and simmer until reduced by half.

**3.** Stir in the date molasses, add the beef stock and bay leaves, then tuck in the browned ribs. The liquid should cover the meat; top it up with more stock or water if needed. Bring to a simmer, cover and transfer to the oven. Braise for 2½–3 hours until the meat is soft and falling off the bone.

**4.** Once the ribs are ready, lift them out and shred the meat with two forks, discarding the bones. Return the meat to the pan, stir it through and taste and adjust the seasoning.

**5.** Cook the rigatoni in salted boiling water until al dente. Drain and stir into the ragù. Let everything bubble together for 2–3 minutes so the pasta sucks up the flavour.

**6.** Serve in big bowls with a handful of chopped herbs and a shower of Parmesan (if using).

DRIED PASTA

# Isle of Wight Harissa Puttanesca

V (without anchovies)/ DF

This is all about the tomatoes. Isle of Wight tomatoes bring sun-soaked sweetness, harissa adds a gentle kick and the briny olives and capers do what they always do best: punch up the flavour. This one's all about balance. Serve with crusty bread and a chilled glass of something dry and white. Or not – you do you.

**SERVES 4**
**PREP TIME: 10 MINS**
**COOK TIME: 50 MINS**

### INGREDIENTS

- 500g Isle of Wight tomatoes, quartered (or halved if small)
- 4 tbsp olive oil, plus extra as needed
- 1–2 tsp chilli flakes (or to taste)
- 4 garlic cloves, thinly sliced
- 2 tbsp harissa paste
- 4–5 anchovy fillets, finely chopped (optional)
- 1 tbsp tomato purée
- 100g pitted black olives, halved
- 2 tbsp capers
- Zest of 1 lemon
- Sea salt and black pepper

### TO SERVE

- 300–400g pasta (spaghetti, linguine or rigatoni work well)
- Fresh oregano or basil, chopped or torn
- Extra virgin olive oil, for drizzling

### METHOD

**1.** Preheat the oven to 180°C fan (200°C/400°F).

**2.** Chuck the quartered tomatoes on a roasting tray, drizzle with a tablespoon of the olive oil, season well and roast for 30 minutes until soft, blistered and caramelised. Once slightly cooled, blitz them in a food processor or blender with all the roasting juices, the chilli flakes, a touch more olive oil and a pinch of salt until smooth. Taste and add more chilli and seasoning if needed. Your roasted tomato passata is now ready.

**3.** Heat the remaining 3 tablespoons of olive oil in a large pan over a medium heat. Add the garlic and let it gently sizzle for 1–2 minutes without browning. Stir in the harissa and cook it out for a couple of minutes until it smells great. Add the anchovies (if using) and let them melt into the oil. Add the tomato purée, cook for a minute, then tip in the roasted passata. Stir, bring it to a simmer and let it bubble away for 10–15 minutes.

**4.** Now throw in the olives and capers. Taste and season – remember the olives and capers bring salt, so don't go mad. Simmer for another 5–7 minutes to let it all come together. Finish with lemon zest and a grind of black pepper.

**5.** While the sauce is doing its thing, cook your pasta in salted boiling water until al dente. Drain, reserving half a mug of pasta water. Toss the pasta straight into the sauce and loosen with a splash of the pasta water if needed. Stir well so it's all coated and glossy.

**6.** Serve with a scatter of oregano or basil and a final drizzle of good olive oil.

DRIED PASTA

# Grated Tomato, Garlic + Feta Pasta

V

Passed down from Jonathan's incredible mother, this is hands-down the quickest and easiest of pastas. No sauce bubbling away, no oven blasting, just a bowl of juicy tomatoes, sharp garlic, salty feta and a squeeze of lemon. It's fresh, tangy, herby and – best of all – it's meant to be eaten at room temperature. Think of it as pasta's answer to a tomato salad. It's sunshine food.

**SERVES 2–3**
**PREP TIME: 10 MINS**
**COOK TIME: 8–10 MINS**

### INGREDIENTS
- 300g ripe vine tomatoes
- 1 garlic clove
- 3 tbsp good olive oil, plus extra for drizzling
- Juice of ½ lemon
- 1 tbsp chopped fresh oregano
- 200g pasta (linguine or fusilli work well)
- 100g feta, crumbled
- 1 tsp za'atar spice blend (optional, but excellent)
- Sea salt and black pepper

### METHOD

**1.** Grate the tomatoes into a bowl using the coarse side of a box grater. You'll be left with a pulpy, saucy mess. Strain it gently through a sieve to get rid of some of the water; you want flavour, not soup.

**2.** Grate the garlic straight into the strained tomatoes. Add the olive oil, lemon juice and chopped oregano and season with salt and pepper. Stir well and let it sit while you cook the pasta.

**3.** Cook your pasta in salted boiling water until just al dente. Drain, then toss the pasta with the tomato mixture until coated. It should look glossy and lightly dressed, not gloopy.

**4.** Top with the crumbled feta, a drizzle of olive oil and a sprinkle of za'atar (if using).

**DRIED PASTA**

# Pasta a la Giada

V (if using vegetarian Parmesan-style cheese or Grana Padano)

This one's from Giada, Nitai's incredible Italian wife and let us tell you, she knows her way around pasta. It's a weeknight hero, a kid pleaser, and has just the right amount of indulgence to make everyone at the table smile. The texture is creamy and risotto-like, and it comes together in minutes.

**SERVES 2–3**
**PREP TIME: 5 MINS**
**COOK TIME: 10 MINS**

### INGREDIENTS
- 200g short pasta (orzo is perfect)
- 2 tbsp mascarpone or cream cheese
- 100g Parmesan or Grana Padano, finely grated
- 1 large egg yolk
- Pinch of chilli flakes (optional)
- Fresh chives, finely chopped
- Sea salt and black pepper

### METHOD

**1.** Bring a large pan of salted water to the boil and cook your pasta until al dente; orzo takes about 8 minutes but check the instructions on the packet. Before draining, scoop out about half a mug of the pasta water and set it aside. Drain the pasta and get ready to mix.

**2.** Off the heat, return the pan to the heat and add the reserved pasta water, mascarpone and half the Parmesan. Whisk it together until smooth and glossy. Throw the pasta back into the pan and stir fast – you want every grain of pasta coated.

**3.** Now take it off the heat completely and stir in the egg yolk, working quickly so it doesn't scramble. Add the rest of the Parmesan and give it a good mix until it's velvety and lush. Season to taste; it might not need salt, but a grind of black pepper never hurts.

**4.** Plate up straight away and finish with a pinch of chilli flakes if you like a bit of heat and a sprinkle of chopped chives.

DRIED PASTA

# Flour & Bread

*always in the pantry*

---

Let's be honest, flour and bread could *each* have their own book. But for now, they're sharing a home here. Flour is one of those ingredients that's so basic, so familiar, you almost forget how magic it is. But take it away and the kitchen crumbles. No bread, no cake, no pastry. No life, basically.

Flour is the foundation of so many things we love at Farmer J – golden, flaky borekas, pillowy soft pitta, croutons fried in butter... Then there's the bread; humble, glorious bread. From herby focaccias to za'atar-dusted flatbread to challah, it turns pantry staples into meals and salads into feasts.

This isn't a sourdough manifesto or a laminated pastry masterclass. These are the real-deal flour and bread recipes we actually cook. The stuff we make at home when we want something warm, nostalgic and properly satisfying.

Expect crisp edges, chewy middles, buttery tops and the smell of something brilliant coming out of the oven.

# Classic Green Salad + Butter Sourdough Croutons

V

Let's talk about croutons; they might just be the unsung hero of the pantry. This recipe is so easy but so good I had to find a place for it. Once you've had croutons fried in butter, you'll never look at a packet of ready-made ones again. These are rich, crisp and salty with a chew in the middle. We toss them into this simple green salad, which is actually my go-to. Butter lettuce is delicate, soft and gives just enough bite, and the vinaigrette is a proper classic – mustardy, sharp and just sweet enough.

**SERVES 4**
**PREP TIME: 15 MINS**
**COOK TIME: 10 MINS**

## INGREDIENTS
- 1 head of butter lettuce, washed and torn into bite-sized leaves
- Handful of fresh dill, roughly chopped
- 1 ripe avocado, sliced (optional)

FOR THE BUTTER SOURDOUGH CROUTONS
- 150g sourdough bread
- 100g unsalted butter
- 1 tbsp olive oil
- Sea salt and black pepper

FOR THE MUSTARD VINAIGRETTE
- 3 tbsp olive oil
- 1 tbsp white wine vinegar (or apple cider vinegar)
- 1 tbsp rice wine vinegar
- 1 tsp Dijon mustard
- 1 tsp pomegranate molasses or maple syrup
- Small handful of fresh dill, finely chopped

## METHOD

**1.** First make the croutons. Cut or tear the sourdough into chunky, rustic croutons. Heat the butter and olive oil in a frying pan over a medium heat. Once melted, toss in the bread and fry gently for 8–10 minutes, stirring often, until golden and crisp on all sides. Season well and let cool in a colander or on kitchen paper. Don't skip this; cooling gives them their crunch.

**2.** While that's happening, whisk up the dressing. Combine the olive oil, vinegars, Dijon mustard, pomegranate molasses or maple syrup, chopped dill and a good pinch of salt and pepper in a small jar or bowl. Shake or whisk until emulsified and glossy.

**3.** In a big bowl, toss the butter lettuce and dill with some of the vinaigrette. Don't overdress; you want it to lightly coat the leaves, not drown them.

**4.** Top with the cooled, crunchy croutons just before serving. If using avocado, gently fan the slices over the top. Add an extra drizzle of dressing if it needs it.

FLOUR & BREAD

# Spinach + Feta Boreka Pie
V

We love a boreka. Or boureka. Or borek. Whatever you call them, they're delicious. This version is our take on the classic Middle Eastern hand pie, sort of a Middle Eastern Cornish pasty. Traditionally, borekas are little flaky parcels filled with cheese, spinach or potato, found everywhere in the Middle East. We've taken that idea and gone bigger, turned it into a showstopper of a pie. Crisp, golden filo, a cheesy spinach centre, and that irresistible sesame top. Basically, a pie you'll want to eat hot, cold, or straight from the tin.

**SERVES 6–8**
**PREP TIME: 20 MINS**
**COOK TIME: 45 MINS**

## INGREDIENTS
- Olive oil, for sautéing and brushing
- 1 garlic clove, thinly sliced
- 1 small-medium white onion, thinly sliced
- 500g spinach
- 350ml whole milk
- 2 eggs
- ¼ tsp grated nutmeg
- 300g pack filo pastry
- 200g feta cheese, crumbled
- 100g mozzarella cheese, grated
- 1 tbsp white sesame seeds
- 1 tbsp black sesame seeds
- Sea salt and black pepper

## METHOD

**1.** Preheat the oven to 170°C fan (190°C/375°F).

**2.** Heat 4 tablespoons of olive oil in a pan over a medium heat. Add the garlic and onion and cook for about 5 minutes until soft but not coloured. Add the spinach and cook for 3–5 minutes until just wilted. Season with salt and pepper, remove from the heat and let it cool.

**3.** In a bowl, whisk together the milk, eggs, nutmeg, a glug of olive oil, a pinch of salt and a few grinds of black pepper.

**4.** Lightly oil a 24cm non-stick springform cake tin. Take four sheets of filo and lay them into the tin, overlapping them and letting the edges hang over the sides (these will form the top later). Dip another four filo sheets into the milk mixture, one at a time, and layer them into the tin over the base.

**5.** Tip in the spinach mixture, spreading it out evenly. Scatter the crumbled feta and grated mozzarella on top. Dip two more filo sheets into the milk mixture and lay them on top of the filling. Pour over any remaining milk mixture.

**6.** Fold the overhanging filo edges inwards to cover the top, brush with a little olive oil and sprinkle with the sesame seeds.

**7.** Bake for about 35 minutes until golden, crisp and the top is puffed and crisp. Let it sit for 5–10 minutes before slicing. Serve warm or at room temperature.

FLOUR & BREAD

# Za'atar 'Pizza'

Ve / DF

We love bread. Flatbread? Even better. This is our Middle Eastern answer to pizza: warm, chewy dough topped with herby, nutty za'atar and good olive oil. We love it for breakfast, with eggs or labneh, or just ripped into as part of a mezze spread. Call it pizza, call it breakfast, just make it.

**MAKES 20 MINI PIZZAS OR 8 LARGE ONES**
**PREP TIME: 40 MINS (PLUS PROVING AND CHILLING)**
**COOK TIME: 8–10 MINS**

### INGREDIENTS
- 675g strong pizza/bread flour
- 13g fine sea salt
- 5g caster sugar
- 7g active dried yeast
- 45ml olive oil
- 450ml ice-cold water

FOR THE TOPPING
- 5 tbsp za'atar spice blend
- 2–3 tbsp olive oil, or enough to make a paste

### METHOD

**1.** Chuck the flour, salt, sugar, yeast, olive oil and ice water into the bowl of a stand mixer fitted with a dough hook (or a large bowl if mixing by hand). Mix on low speed for 4 minutes, then on medium for 5 minutes until smooth, stretchy and glossy. If mixing by hand, mix with a wooden spoon or your hands until it starts to come together, then knead on a clean surface for 10–12 minutes until smooth, stretchy and glossy. Transfer to a large, oiled container, cover and set aside to rest for 30 minutes. Then give it a fold: gently stretch one side of the dough up and fold it over itself, rotate the bowl and repeat three more times – this strengthens the gluten. Cover again and pop it in the fridge overnight.

**2.** The next day, cut the dough into 50g pieces and roll into balls, or divide into eight equal pieces for larger pizzas. Rest them on a tray lined with baking parchment, covered with a tea towel, for 25–30 minutes at room temperature.

**3.** For the topping, stir together the za'atar and olive oil to make a thick paste.

**4.** Once the dough has rested, press and stretch each ball into a flat circle – around 10–12cm in diameter for small ones, or 25–28cm for large ones – with your fingertips. Spoon and spread the za'atar paste all over. Let the topped dough rest again for 10 minutes.

**5.** Preheat the oven to 250°C fan (270°C/510°F). If you've got a pizza stone, now is its time to shine. Bake the pizzas for 8–10 minutes until puffed and golden on the edges.

# Olive Oil Cake + Rose Water cream

V

This is Nitai's famous cake. Moist, zesty olive oil sponge with a silky rose water cream and crunchy, buttery kadaifi on top, it's outrageous. But honestly, the cake on its own is incredible. You can serve it plain with a cup of tea, or dress it up with the cream, pistachio sauce and kadaifi if you fancy. Most of the extras can be made ahead and assembled just before serving.

**SERVES 12–16**
**PREP TIME: 30 MINS (PLUS COOLING)**
**COOK TIME: 1 HOUR 15 MINS**

**INGREDIENTS**
- 4 large eggs
- 400ml whole milk
- 375ml olive oil
- Zest of 1 lemon
- 475g plain flour
- 450g caster sugar
- 1 tsp bicarbonate of soda
- 1 tsp baking powder
- ½ tsp fine sea salt

FOR THE ROSE WATER CREAM
- 500ml whole milk
- 100g caster sugar
- 30g cornflour
- 4 egg yolks
- 1–2 tsp rose water (more if you love it)
- 250ml double cream, whipped to soft peaks
- 1 tsp vanilla bean paste

FOR THE PISTACHIOS
- 200g shelled pistachios, divided
  - 100g for sugaring
  - 100g for toasting and crumbling

FOR THE SUGARED PISTACHIOS
- 60g caster sugar
- 1½ tbsp water

FOR THE KADAIFI CRUMBLE
- 350g kadaifi pastry or shredded filo
- 100g icing sugar
- 140g melted butter
- 100g sugared pistachios (from above)
- 100g plain toasted pistachios (from above)
- 2 tbsp dried rose petals (optional)
- ½ tsp sea salt

FOR THE PISTACHIO SAUCE (OPTIONAL)
- 300ml double cream
- 100g caster sugar
- 4 egg yolks
- 80g pistachio paste

## METHOD

**1.** Preheat the oven to 160°C fan (180°C/350°F) and line a 23 x 33cm baking tray with baking parchment.

**2.** In a large bowl, whisk the eggs, milk, olive oil and lemon zest. In another bowl, mix the flour, sugar, bicarb, baking powder and salt. Fold the dry ingredients into the wet until you have a smooth batter.

**3.** Pour into the lined tray and bake for 35-40 minutes, or until a skewer comes out clean. Check after 30 minutes and cover with foil if it's browning too quickly. Cool completely on a wire rack.

**4.** For the rose water cream, heat the milk until steaming. In a bowl, whisk the sugar, cornflour and egg yolks, then slowly whisk in the warm milk. Return to the pan and cook until thick, then stir in the rose water. Chill with cling film pressed directly on top. Once cold, fold in the whipped cream and vanilla bean paste.

**5.** Toast all 200g pistachios on a tray in the oven for 8-10 minutes. Set aside 100g for the crumble.

**6.** To make the sugared pistachios, simmer the sugar and water in a small pan, then stir in the remaining 100g toasted pistachios until the sugar crystallises. Spread on baking paper to cool.

**7.** Shred the kadaifi by hand, then mix with icing sugar and melted butter. Spread on a tray and bake at 170°C fan (190°C/375°F) for 30-40 minutes, tossing every 10-12 minutes, until golden and crisp. Cool, then toss with 100g sugared pistachios, 100g toasted pistachios, rose petals and salt.

**8.** For the pistachio sauce (if making), gently heat the cream in a pan. In a bowl, whisk the egg yolks and sugar, then slowly add the warm cream. Return to the pan and stir until slightly thickened, then whisk in the pistachio paste.

**9.** To serve, cut the cake into squares. Top with rose water cream, a generous spoon of crumble, a drizzle of pistachio sauce (if using), and a few rose petals if you're feeling fancy.

**FLOUR & BREAD**

# Date Molasses Challah Bread

V

There's nothing quite like the smell of fresh challah filling your kitchen – sweet, golden and slightly sticky from the richness of date molasses. This version has that perfect tear-apart softness with a whisper of deep caramel running through it. It's the kind of bread that gets devoured warm from the oven, slathered in butter, or toasted with jam the next morning. Whether you're making it by hand or giving your mixer a workout, this is one recipe you'll come back to every Friday.

**MAKES 1 LARGE LOAF**
**PREP TIME: 30 MINS (PLUS RESTING AND PROVING)**
**COOK TIME: 25–30 MINS**

## INGREDIENTS
- 430ml ice-cold water
- 1 large egg
- 50ml avocado oil
- 25g date molasses
- 50g caster sugar
- 16g fresh yeast (or 7g active dried yeast)
- 1kg plain flour
- 12g fine sea salt
- 1 egg, beaten with a splash of water

OPTIONAL TOPPINGS
- Sesame seeds (white or black)
- Poppy seeds
- Pumpkin seeds
- Sunflower seeds
- Flaxseeds
- Flaky sea salt

## METHOD

**1.** Start with the wet stuff. In the bowl of a stand mixer (or just a large bowl if you're doing it by hand), whisk together the water, egg, oil, date molasses, sugar and yeast. Let it sit for 5–10 minutes until it looks a bit foamy – this tells you that the yeast is alive and kicking.

**2.** Add the flour and salt, then if you're using a stand mixer, knead with a dough hook on low speed for 3 minutes to combine. Crank it up to medium speed and knead for another 5 minutes until the dough is soft, smooth and just a bit tacky. Doing it by hand? Tip it out on to a floured surface and knead for about 10–12 minutes, or until your arms feel like they've earned a rest. Pop the dough into a lightly oiled bowl and cover with a tea towel. Let it rest for 30 minutes, then give it a quick fold by pulling the edges into the centre like a parcel. Do this two more times, every 30 minutes. Then cover it up and stick it in the fridge overnight or leave to prove at room temperature for 3 hours.

**3.** When you're ready to shape, divide the dough into four equal balls, around 395g each. Let them rest for 20 minutes under a tea towel.

**4.** Roll each dough ball into a long rope about 26cm long with slightly tapered ends, then braid into a four-strand challah. Tuck the ends under and place on a baking tray lined with baking parchment.

**5.** Brush the loaf generously with the egg wash right after shaping. This gives you that deep, shiny crust. Leave it to prove at room temperature for 40 minutes until puffed. Towards the end of this last prove, preheat the oven to 180°C fan (200°C/400°F). Brush the bread with more egg wash and sprinkle with whatever toppings you fancy or leave plain.

**6.** Bake the challah for 25–30 minutes, or until golden and glossy and it sounds hollow when tapped underneath. Let it cool a bit if you can resist it, although warm, ripped-apart challah is kind of the point.

FLOUR & BREAD

# Nitai's Basque Labneh Cheesecake

V / GF (use cornflour)

This is one of Nitai's signature bakes – and with good reason. Rich, creamy, tangy and just salty enough, it's got that signature wobble in the middle and a deep, caramelised top that'll make you look like a pastry wizard. The labneh cuts through the richness with a savoury edge that keeps you going back in with your spoon.

**SERVES 10–12**
**PREP TIME: 20 MINS (PLUS CHILLING)**
**COOK TIME: 40 MINS**

### INGREDIENTS

- 375g cream cheese
- 125g Labneh (page 40)
- 110g caster sugar
- Seeds from ½ vanilla pod or ½ tbsp vanilla bean paste
- ½ tsp sea salt
- 3 large eggs
- 200ml double cream
- 12g plain flour or cornflour
- Zest of ½ lemon

### METHOD

**1.** Preheat the oven to 210°C fan (230°C/450°F). This high heat gives the cheesecake its deep brown top.

**2.** In a very large bowl, beat together the cream cheese, labneh, sugar and vanilla until smooth. Add the sea salt and keep mixing. Crack in the eggs one at a time, mixing well after each addition so it stays creamy, not lumpy. Pour in the double cream and mix until silky. Sift in the flour or cornflour and stir just until it disappears. Finally, fold in the lemon zest.

**3.** Line a 20cm springform cake tin with baking parchment, making sure the paper rises at least 5cm above the top of the tin. Pour in the batter and smooth the top.

**4.** Bake for 25 minutes until the top is puffed and deep golden brown. Then reduce the temperature to 150°C fan (170°C/340°F) and bake for another 15 minutes. It should still have a wobble in the middle.

**5.** Let it cool completely at room temperature, then chill in the fridge for at least 4 hours (overnight is best). Slice thick and serve cold. Serve just as it is, or maybe with a simple fruit compote.

FLOUR & BREAD

# Quick dinners

No time? No problem. This is all about those 'what's in the fridge' moments that still need to taste like a win. Whether you've got ten minutes or half an hour, these recipes don't mess around. They're punchy, satisfying and leave you with more time to binge-watch something good while your kitchen still smells like someone cooked. (Which, technically, you did.)

**QUICK DINNER RECIPES**

- Chermoula Fish Skewers with Blistered Greens (page 28)

- Shawarma Shroom Skewers & Spicy Green Tahini (page 55)

- Za'atar Cauli Schnitzel, Caper Mayo & Schug (page 64)

- Seared Tuna with Asian Nori Dukkah & Rice Noodle Salad (page 149)

- Quickie Hummus, Za'atar Aubergine & Soft-boiled Egg (page 205)

- Chickpea Crumble & Cavolo Nero Salad (page 212)

- Sausage, Porcini & Fennel Pasta (page 216)

- Grated Tomato, Garlic & Feta Pasta (page 227)

# Weekend brunch

Brunch is a state of mind. This is the place for late mornings, strong coffee and a table full of bits. These recipes are relaxed but still impressive, the kind of thing you pull together while chatting, half-dressed, with music on and no plan for the rest of the day.

We've got eggs, grains, sweet things, big spreads and spicy sauces that'll wake you up in all the right ways. Brunch should feel like a reward, not a panic. And if it stretches into lunch . . . even better.

|  | RECIPES | WHY IT WORKS |
|---|---|---|
| **BRUNCH ONE** | <ul><li>Herb Frittata with Preserved Lemon & Feta (page 177)</li><li>Avocado Toast with Preserved Lemon, Chilli & Coriander (page 176)</li><li>labneh and pickles</li></ul> | Bright, herby, and creamy. |
| **BRUNCH TWO** | <ul><li>Harissa Shakshuka & Fresh Market Salad (page 48)</li><li>Green Chickpea Masabacha (page 206)</li><li>Chocolate Tahini Challah Bread Pudding (page 93)</li><li>piles of pitta or fresh challah</li></ul> | Spicy, creamy, sweet and soft – the shakshuka brings heat, the pudding brings indulgence, and the pitta ties it all together. |
| **BRUNCH THREE** | <ul><li>Spinach & Feta Boreka Pie (page 232)</li><li>scrambled eggs</li></ul> | A flaky, cheesy pie with punchy salad and eggs is peak 'brunch at home' comfort. |
| **BRUNCH FIVE** | <ul><li>Green Za'atar Shakshuka (page 61)</li><li>Smashed Cucumber Salad with Sesame Miso Tahini Dressing (page 154)</li><li>Sesame Milk Bun Bagels (page 155)</li></ul> | This one's fresh, funky and bold – hot shakshuka, cold cucumber and chewy bagels for the perfect scooping vehicle. |
| **BRUNCH SIX** | <ul><li>Grilled Cheese Toastie with Onion Marmalade & Yeast Extract Butter (page 117)</li><li>Harissa Fennel Salad (page 42)</li></ul> | Crispy, melty toastie with sharp salad on the side. |

# Balanced plates and tables

Proper meals, built around the Fieldtray philosophy. A base, a main, a side (maybe two if you're feeling generous) and a punchy sauce or salad to tie it all together. These are plates that take a bit more time than our quick dinners but still respect your evening. They're hearty but never heavy, balanced without being boring, and built with flavour at the core. Whether it's a Tuesday dinner that turns into a feast, or a buffet table for a crowd, this section's all about the sweet spot between bold and doable.

| | COMPONENTS | WHY IT WORKS |
|---|---|---|
| **PLATE ONE**<br>The Classic<br>Farmer J | • Farmer's Grains (*page 197*)<br>• Harissa Chicken Thighs (*page 44*)<br>• Spiced Baharat Sweet Potatoes (*page 19*)<br>• Charred Sesame Broccoli (*page 151*)<br>• or Mac and Cheese (*page 218*) | A classic at Farmer J – spicy, comforting, balanced and customisable with bold sauces or creamy sides. |
| **PLATE TWO**<br>Chicken + Cauli | • Freekeh Tabouleh (*page 198*)<br>• Chermoula Chicken & Pickle Plate (*page 30*)<br>• Whole Roasted Harissa Cauliflower & Spicy Green Tahini (*page 47*) | Punchy chicken meets smoky cauliflower and bright freekeh. |
| **PLATE THREE**<br>Gochujang<br>Sticky Salmon<br>Bowl | • Sticky Salmon Rice Bowl (*page 187*)<br>• Coconut Rice (*page 152*)<br>• Smashed Cucumber Salad (*page 67*)<br>• Kale Miso Slaw (*page 101*) | A full rice bowl built for impact – hot, cold, crunchy and sticky all in one dish. |
| **PLATE FOUR**<br>Amba<br>Chicken Plate | • Amba Chicken Thighs (*page 71*)<br>• Spicy Green Tahini (*page 83*)<br>• Charred Courgette, Preserved Lemon, Mint & Pine Nuts (*page 181*)<br>• Farmer's Grains (*page 197*) | A proper feel-good dinner plate with balance and depth. |
| **PLATE FIVE**<br>Chickpea<br>Fish Stew<br>Plate | • Chickpea Fish Stew (*page 210*)<br>• Roasted Leeks & Dukkah Crumble (*page 144*)<br>• Shaved Winter Greens & Coriander Vinaigrette (*page 164*) | Warming stew, creamy leeks and crisp greens – this one's got richness, freshness and crunch where you need it. |

**MEAL PLANS**

# Farmer J feasts

Big flavours. Big energy. Big reasons to gather. Whether it's Christmas, a birthday, or just a Saturday night with mates, these are the meals you pull out when you want to impress *and* eat well. This section's full of bold flavours and proper party energy, without sending you into meltdown (hopefully).

We're talking slow roasts, punchy sauces, statement salads, trays of indulgent sides and the odd outrageous dessert. Some are a full sit-down spread, others are more 'graze and chat'. Enjoy.

| | RECIPES | WHY IT WORKS |
|---|---|---|
| **FEAST ONE**<br>A Festive Alternative | • Baharat Sticky Salmon (*page 22*)<br>• Roasted Brussels Sprouts with Miso-Maple-Tahini (*page 100*)<br>• Roasted Cabbage with Yeast Extract (*page 120*)<br>• **OR** Whole Roast Celeriac (*page 87*)<br>• Castelfranco Salad (*page 135*)<br>• Honey, Tahini & Olive Oil Bundt (*page 94*) | Big, comforting and dramatic enough for a festive table. Every dish sings and the bundt is a brilliant finish. |
| **FEAST TWO**<br>A Summer Mediterranean Spread | • Yellow Courgette, Green Bean & Za'atar Salad (*page 62*)<br>• Grilled Peaches (*page 109*)<br>• Kohlrabi Carpaccio (*page 136*)<br>• Grated Tomato, Garlic + Feta Pasta (*page 227*)<br>• Harissa Puttanesca (*page 224*)<br>• Chocolate Tahini Tiramisu (*page 90*) | Light, summery and vibrant, perfect for long lunches, garden dinners, or sun-drenched birthdays. |
| **FEAST THREE**<br>Easy Party with Friends | • Slow-cooked Lamb Shoulder & All the Toppings (*page 56*) | Just one showstopper – minimal fuss, major flavour, made for sharing. |
| **FEAST FOUR**<br>Dirty but Delicious | • Yeast Extract Baharat Chicken Wings (*page 115*)<br>• Dips & Chips (*page 128*)<br>• **OR** Pulled Lamb with Pitta Chip 'Nachos' (*page 130*)<br>• Farmer J Mac (*page 218*) | Sticky, crispy, cheesy and full of joy. |

**MEAL PLANS**

**FEAST FIVE**
Just Bites, All Punch

- Stuffed Pitta & Alice's Yoghurt Leeks *(page 76)*
- Leek & Chicken Kofta & Tzatziki *(page 74)*
- Kalamata Gilda *(page 167)*
  Tommy's Freekancini *(page 201)*
- Za'atar 'Pizza' *(page 234)*
- Charred Corn Ribs & Gochujang Mayo *(page 192)*

Perfect party food, bold, bite-sized and absolutely packed with flavour. Great for grazing all night.

# Conversion tables

**WEIGHTS ***

| METRIC | IMPERIAL |
|---|---|
| 15 g | 1/2 oz |
| 25 g | 1 oz |
| 40 g | 1½ oz |
| 50 g | 2 oz |
| 75 g | 3 oz |
| 100 g | 4 oz |
| 150 g | 5 oz |
| 175 g | 6 oz |
| 200 g | 7 oz |
| 225 g | 8 oz |
| 250 g | 9 oz |
| 275 g | 10 oz |
| 350 g | 12 oz |
| 375 g | 13 oz |
| 400 g | 14 oz |
| 425 g | 15 oz |
| 450 g | 1 lb |
| 550 g | 1¼ lb |
| 675 g | 1½ lb |
| 900 g | 2 lb |
| 1.5 kg | 3 lb |
| 1.75 kg | 4 lb |
| 2.25 kg | 5 lb |

* 28.35g = 1oz but the measurements here have been rounded up or down to make conversion easier

**VOLUME**

| METRIC | IMPERIAL |
|---|---|
| 25 ml | 1 fl oz |
| 50 ml | 2 fl oz |
| 85 ml | 3 fl oz |
| 150 ml | 5 fl oz (¼ pint) |
| 300 ml | 10 fl oz (¼ pint) |
| 450 ml | 15 fl oz (¾ pint) |
| 600 ml | 1 pint |
| 700 ml | 1¼ pints |
| 900 ml | 1½ pints |
| 1 litre | 1¾ pints |
| 1.2 litres | 2 pints |
| 1.25 litres | 2¼ pints |
| 1.5 litres | 2½ pints |
| 1.6 litres | 2¾ pints |
| 1.75 litres | 3 pints |
| 1.8 litres | 3¼ pints |
| 2 litres | 3½ pints |
| 2.1 litres | 3¾ pints |
| 2.25 litres | 4 pints |
| 2.75 litres | 5 pints |
| 3.4 litres | 6 pints |
| 3.9 litres | 7 pints |
| 5 litres | 8 pints (1 gal) |

**MEASUREMENTS**

| METRIC | IMPERIAL |
|---|---|
| 0.5 cm | ¼ inch |
| 1 cm | ½ inch |
| 2.5 cm | 1 inch |
| 5 cm | 2 inches |
| 7.5 cm | 3 inches |
| 10 cm | 4 inches |
| 15 cm | 6 inches |
| 18 cm | 7 inches |
| 20 cm | 8 inches |
| 23 cm | 9 inches |
| 25 cm | 10 inches |
| 30 cm | 12 inches |

**OVEN TEMPERATURES**

| °C | °F | GAS MK |
|---|---|---|
| 140°C | 275°F | Gas Mk 1 |
| 150°C | 300°F | Gas Mk 2 |
| 160°C | 325°F | Gas Mk 3 |
| 180°C | 350°F | Gas Mk 4 |
| 190°C | 375°F | Gas Mk 5 |
| 200°C | 400°F | Gas Mk 6 |
| 220°C | 425°F | Gas Mk 7 |
| 230°C | 450°F | Gas Mk 8 |
| 240°C | 475°F | Gas Mk 9 |

# Index

Note: page numbers in **bold** refer to illustrations.

## A
aioli 142, **143**
  honey & crème fraîche 142, **143**
  pickled chilli 161
  yeast extract 120, **121**
  yoghurt 19
almond
  almond dukkah 144, **145**
  celeriac-almond cream 203
amba 68–77
artichoke, roasted Jerusalem artichoke + tahini-amba yoghurt 72, **73**
aubergine
  aubergine shawarma pitta 52, **53**
  burnt aubergine, tahini + pistachio 84, **85**
  gochujang aubergine 189
  quickie hummus, za'atar aubergine + soft-boiled egg 205, **205**
  roasted aubergine, hispi cabbage + za'atar chickpeas + spicy aubergine tahini 208–9
  roasted aubergine + tahini yoghurt + brown butter 128
  roasted tofu, hispi + aubergine + smoked chilli miso 102, **103**
avocado toast + preserved lemon, chilli & coriander 176, **179**

## B
bagels 155, **156**
baharat 18–25, 115
banana + date loaf cake 112, **113**
bean(s)
  cavolo nero, butter beans, kalamata + oregano salad 172, **173**
  harissa baked beans, labneh, preserved lemon + poached egg 40, **41**
  tuna, green bean + raw tahini tartare 88, **89**
  yellow courgette, green bean + za'atar salad 62

béchamel sauce 215, 218, **220–1**
beef
  braised short rib ragù + rigatoni **222**, 223
  bucatini al forno + Bolognese ragù 215
  stuffed spiced pitta + Alice's yoghurt leeks 76–7, **76**, **78–9**
beetroot 51
  roasted beetroot, freekeh + walnut salad 138
boreka pie, spinach + feta 232, **233**
bread 40, 230–40
  butter sourdough croutons 231
  chocolate tahini challah bread pudding **92**, 93
  panzanella 170, **171**
  see also bagels; pitta; toast; toastie
broccoli 219
  charred sesame broccoli + maple lemon ponzu 151
brunches 244
Brussels sprouts 219
  roasted Brussels sprouts + hispi + miso-maple-tahini 100
butter
  brown 128
  butter sourdough croutons 231
  sage **34**, 35
  yeast extract **116**, 117–18, **119**

## C
cabbage see hispi cabbage; red cabbage; white cabbage
cakes
  banana + date loaf 112, **113**
  honey, tahini + olive oil bundt **94**, 95
  olive oil 236–7, **237**
caper mayo 64, **65**
cauliflower
  freekeh tabouleh + roasted cauliflower 198, **199**
  whole roasted harissa cauliflower + spicy green tahini **46**, 47

  za'atar cauli schnitzel, caper mayo + schug 64, **65**
cavolo nero
  cavolo nero, butter beans, kalamata + oregano salad 172, **173**
  cavolo nero salad 212, **213**
  lamb meatballs + cavolo nero + goat's yoghurt 110, **111**
celeriac
  celeriac-almond cream 203
  whole roast celeriac + celeriac + tahini cream **86**, 87
ceviche, leche de tigre 162, **163**
challah
  chocolate tahini challah bread pudding **92**, 93
  date molasses challah **238**, 239
cheese 219
  Farmer J mac 218, **220–1**
  grilled cheese toastie + onion marmalade + yeast extract butter **116**, 117
  see also feta; mozzarella; Parmesan
cheesecake, Nitai's Basque labneh 240, **241**
chermoula 26–37
chicken
  amba chicken thighs **70**, 71
  chermoula chicken + pickle plate 30–1
  chermoula spatchcock chicken + sage butter potatoes **34**, 35
  classic harissa chicken thighs 44, **45**
  leek + chicken kofta + tzatziki 74, **75**
  sticky chicken thighs + chunky herb slaw 106, **107**
  yeast extract baharat chicken wings 115
chickpea(s) 204–13
  pickled chilli chickpea salad 165
  preserved lemon, chickpea, spinach + Swiss chard stew 180

za'atar chickpeas 62,
  208–9
chilli 176
  pickled chilli 160–5
  pickled chilli aioli 161
  pickled chilli chickpea
    salad 165
  smoked chilli miso 102, **103**
chimichurri 144, **145**
chips
  dips + chips 128–9
  pitta chip 'nachos' 130, **131**
  pitta chips 124–5
chocolate
  chocolate tahini challah
    bread pudding **92**, 93
  chocolate tahini tiramisu
    90–1, **90–1**
coconut lime leaf curry + tofu,
  hispi cabbage + coconut
  rice 152–3, **153**
cookies, tahini walnut 139
coriander
  rice 22, **23**
  vinaigrette 164
corn cobs
  charred corn ribs +
    gochujang mayo 192, **193**
  esquites corn salad 36, **37**
courgette
  charred courgette,
    preserved lemon, mint +
    pine nuts 181
  raw courgette salad +
    lemon vinaigrette +
    dukkah 147
  yellow courgette, green
    bean + za'atar salad 62
cream
  celeriac + tahini **86**, 87
  celeriac-almond 203
  mascarpone 90–1, **90–1**
  rose water 236–7, **237**
croutons, butter sourdough
  231
cucumber
  pickled cucumber 146
  smashed cucumber salad
    + miso tahini ponzu
    dressing 154
  za'atar smashed
    cucumber salad **66**, 67
curry, coconut lime leaf
  152–3, **153**

### D
date + banana loaf cake 112,
  **113**
date molasses 104–112, 133,
  239

dips 128–9, 177, **178**
dressings 138, 146, 170, **171**,
  190, **191**
  Caesar 126, **127**
  honey & crème fraîche
    aioli 142, **143**
  honey walnut **134**, 135
  lemon & oregano 62
  lemon tahini 165
  miso 97
  miso tahini ponzu 154
  niçoise 169
  oregano 172, **173**
  sweet white miso 101
  tahini Caesar 212, **213**
dukkah 140–9
  almond dukkah 144, **145**
  Asian nori dukkah 141
  classic dukkah 141
  shawarma roasted roots,
    feta + dukkah 51

### E
egg 52, 201
  Farmer J niçoise 169
  green za'atar shakshuka
    61, **157**
  harissa shakshuka 48, **49**
  herb frittata 177, **178**
  poached egg 40, **41**
  quickie hummus, za'atar
    aubergine + soft-boiled
    egg 205, **205**
  soy-cured egg yolk 98, **99**
endive 135, 169
  citrus endive dukkah salad
    142, **143**
equipment 14–15
esquites corn salad 36, **37**

### F
fennel
  harissa fennel salad 42
  sausage, porcini + fennel
    pasta 216, **217**
feta 48, 61, 167, 198, 201, 219
  grated tomato, garlic + feta
    pasta **226**, 227
  herb frittata + preserved
    lemon + feta 177, **178**
  shawarma roasted roots,
    feta + dukkah 51
  spinach + feta boreka pie
    232, **233**
Fieldtrays 7
fish
  chermoula fish skewers +
    blistered greens + lemon
    zest 28, **29**
  chickpea fish stew 210, **211**

leche de tigre ceviche +
  pickled red onion 162,
  **163**
*see also* salmon; tuna
freekeh 196–203
  roasted beetroot, freekeh +
    walnut salad 138
  Tommy's freekancini **76**,
    **78–9**, 201
frittata, herb 177, **178**

### G
Giada, pasta a la 228, **229**
Gilda, kalamata 167, **168**
gochujang 184–92
  gochujang mayo 192, **193**
grains, Farmer's 197
greens
  blistered 28, **29**
  green za'atar shakshuka
    61, **157**
  shaved winter 164

### H
harissa 38–48, 129, 224
hawaij spice blend 69
hispi cabbage 146
  coconut lime leaf curry +
    hispi cabbage 152–3,
    **153**
  roasted aubergine + hispi
    cabbage 208–9
  roasted Brussels sprouts +
    hispi 100
  roasted cabbage, yeast
    extract aioli + pickled kale
    120, **121**
  roasted tofu + hispi 102,
    **103**
honey
  honey & crème fraîche
    aioli dressing 142, **143**
  honey, tahini + olive oil
    bundt 94, **95**
  honey walnut dressing **134**,
    135
  smokey honey harissa 43
hummus, quickie 205, **205**

### K
kadaifi crumble 236–7,
  **237**
kale 219
  kale Caesar 126, **127**
  kale miso slaw 101
  pickled kale 120, **121**
kofta, leek + chicken 74, **75**
kohlrabi carpaccio + sesame
  + Parmesan 136, **137**

**L**

labneh
　labneh + harissa baked beans 40, **41**
　labneh dip 177, **178**
　Nitai's Basque labneh cheesecake 240, **241**
lamb
　baharat roasted lamb shanks + mint schug 20–1, **21**
　chermoula lamb chops + mint yoghurt 32, **33**
　lamb meatballs + cavolo nero + goat's yoghurt 110, **111**
　pulled lamb + pitta chip 'nachos' 130, **131**
　slow-cooked lamb shanks + yeast extract butter potatoes 118, **119**
　slow-cooked lamb shoulder + all the toppings 56–7, **58–9**
leche de tigre ceviche 162, **163**
leek 219
　Alice's yoghurt leeks 76–7, **76**, **78–9**
　leek + chicken kofta + tzatziki 74, **75**
　roasted leeks + dukkah crumble 144, **145**
lemon
　lemon & oregano dressing 62
　lemon tahini dressing 165
　lemon vinaigrette 147
　maple lemon ponzu 151
lemon (preserved) 40, 174–82
　preserved lemon tart 182, **183**
lime & dill vinaigrette 147
lime leaf coconut curry 152–3, **153**

**M**

mac and cheese 218, **220–1**
maple syrup
　maple lemon ponzu 151
　miso-maple-tahini 100
marmalade, onion **116**, 117
masabacha, green chickpea 206, **207**
mascarpone cream 90–1, **90–1**
mayo
　caper 64, **65**
　gochujang 192, **193**

meal plans 242–7
mint
　charred courgette + mint 181
　mint schug 20–1, **21**
　mint yoghurt 32, **33**
miso 96–102
　miso gochujang sauce 189
　miso tahini ponzu dressing 154
mozzarella, grilled peaches, mozzarella, date molasses + basil **108**, 109
mushroom 219
　a lot of mushrooms + miso dressing 98, **99**
　mushroom + freekeh risotto + skordalia **202**, 203
　sausage, porcini + fennel pasta 216, **217**
　shawarma shroom skewers + spicy green tahini 54, **55**
mustard vinaigrette 231

**N**

'nachos', pitta chip 130, **131**
noodles
　gochujang prawns + rice noodles 190, **191**
　rice noodle salad 148, 149
nori, Asian nori dukkah 141, **148**, 149

**O**

olive oil cake + rose water cream 236–7, **237**
olive(s), kalamata 166–73, 219
onion
　crispy 105
　onion marmalade **116**, 117
　pickled red 62, 160–5, 162, **163**
　stuffed onions tahini sauce 200
　sumac 56–7, **58–9**
oregano dressing 172, **173**
orzo, pasta a la Giada 228, **229**
ox cheek, baharat + beer-braised ox cheeks 24, 25

**P**

panzanella 170, **171**
Parmesan 201, 219, 228
　kohlrabi carpaccio + sesame + Parmesan 136, **137**
　potatoes 57, **58–9**

pasta 214–28
pastry dishes 182, **183**, 232, **233**
peach, grilled peaches, mozzarella, date molasses + basil **108**, 109
pepper 48, 170, 219
　smoky roasted red pepper + walnut dip 129
pickles 159–92
　pickle plate 30–1
　pickled chilli 160–5
　pickled chilli aioli 161
　pickled chilli chickpea salad 165
　pickled cucumber 146
　pickled kale 120, **121**
　pickled red onion 62, 160–5, 162, **163**
　quick-pickled red cabbage 101
pie, spinach + feta boreka 232, **233**
pistachio
　burnt aubergine, tahini + pistachio 84, **85**
　pistachio sauce 236–7, **237**
pitta
　aubergine shawarma 52, **53**
　pitta chip 'nachos' 130, **131**
　pitta chips 124–5
　stuffed spiced pitta 76–7, **76**, **78–9**
'pizza', za'atar 234, **235**
ponzu
　maple lemon ponzu 151
　miso tahini ponzu dressing 154
potato 52, 169
　Parmesan potatoes 57, **58–9**
　sage butter **34**, 35
　yeast extract butter 118, **119**
prawn, gochujang prawns + rice noodles 190, **191**
puttanesca 224, **225**

**Q**

quick dinner recipes 243

**R**

ragù
　braised short rib ragù + rigatoni **222**, 223
　bucatini al forno + Bolognese ragù 215
red cabbage
　quick-pickled 101
　slaws 101, 106, **107**

rice
   coconut rice 152, **153**
   coriander rice 22, **23**
   sticky salmon rice bowl **186**, 187
risotto, mushroom + freekeh risotto + skordalia **202**, 203
roots, shawarma roasted roots, feta + dukkah 51
rose water cream 236–7, **237**

## S

sage butter potatoes **34**, 35
salads 7
   cabbage 57, **58–9**
   Castelfranco **134**, 135
   cavolo nero, butter beans, kalamata + oregano 172, **173**
   chickpea crumble + cavolo nero 212, **213**
   citrus endive dukkah 142, **143**
   classic green 231
   esquites corn 36, **37**
   Farmer J niçoise 169
   fresh market 48, **49**
   harissa fennel 42
   kale Caesar 126, **127**
   panzanella 170, **171**
   pickled chilli chickpea 165
   raw courgette 147
   rice noodle **148**, 149
   roasted beetroot, freekeh + walnut 138
   smashed cucumber **66**, 67, 154
   yellow courgette, green bean + za'atar 62
   za'atar smashed cucumber **66**, 67
salmon
   baharat sticky salmon + coriander rice 22, **23**
   sticky salmon rice bowl **186**, 187
sausage, porcini + fennel pasta 216, **217**
schug 64, **65**
   mint 20–1, **21**
   Nitai's 63
sesame seed 136, 150–5
shakshuka
   green za'atar 61, **157**
   harissa 48, **49**
shawarma 50–7
skordalia + mushroom + freekeh risotto **202**, 203
slaw
   chunky herb 106, **107**
   green dukkah 146
   kale miso 101
soy-cured egg yolk 98, **99**
spinach
   preserved lemon, chickpea, spinach + Swiss chard stew 180
   spinach + feta boreka pie 232, **233**
stews
   chickpea fish 210, **211**
   preserved lemon, chickpea, spinach + Swiss chard 180
sumac onions 56–7, **58–9**
sweet potato
   smashed sweet potatoes + date molasses tahini + crispy onions 105
   spiced baharat sweet potatoes + yoghurt aioli 19
   sweet potato purée 162, **163**
Swiss chard, preserved lemon, chickpea + spinach stew 180

## T

tabouleh, freekeh 198, **199**
tahini 82–94
   beetroot & walnut tahini spread 138
   date molasses tahini 105
   lemon tahini dressing 165
   miso tahini ponzu dressing 154
   miso-maple-tahini 100
   quickie hummus 205, **205**
   spicy aubergine tahini 208–9
   spicy green tahini **46**, 47, **54**, 55, 83
   tahini Caesar dressing 212, **213**
   tahini sauce 200
   tahini walnut cookies 139
   tahini yoghurt 128
   tahini-amba yoghurt 72, **73**
tart, preserved lemon 182, **183**
tartare, tuna 88, **89**
tiramisu, chocolate tahini 90–1, **90–1**
toast, avocado 176, **179**
toastie, cheese **116**, 117
tofu
   coconut lime leaf curry + tofu 152–3, **153**
   roasted tofu, hispi + aubergine + smoked chilli miso 102, **103**
tomato 48, 172, 219, 224
   grated tomato, garlic + feta pasta **226**, 227
   heritage tomato + kalamata panzanella 170, **171**
   spicy tomatoes 57, **58–9**
tuna
   Farmer J niçoise 169
   green bean + raw tahini tartare 88, **89**
   seared tuna + Asian nori dukkah + rice noodle salad **148**, 149
tzatziki 74, **75**

## V

vegetables, seasonal 219
vinaigrette
   coriander 164
   harissa 42
   lemon 147
   lime & dill 147
   mustard 231

## W

walnut 129, 132–9
white cabbage 164
   cabbage salad 57, **58**
   roasted cabbage, yeast extract aioli + pickled kale 120, **121**
   slaws 101, 106, **107**

## Y

yeast extract 114–20
yoghurt
   Alice's yoghurt leeks 76–7, **76**, 78–9
   harissa yoghurt dip 129
   lamb meatballs + cavolo nero + goat's yoghurt 110, **111**
   mint yoghurt 32, **33**
   tahini yoghurt 128
   tahini-amba yoghurt 72, **73**
   yoghurt aioli 19

## Z

za'atar 60–7, 133, 205, 208–9, 234

# From Ali

First, to Jonathan. Without you, there'd be no Farmer J. You are the captain of the ship, the vision, the drive, the reason any of this exists. You're a proper leader and you keep this thing moving forward even when the seas are rough. I love you.

To Nitai, what a man. What a chef. What a teammate. This book would be about 20 pages without you and a whole lot duller. You've brought the flavour, the finesse and the obsession. Watching you in the kitchen is magic. Eating your food? Even better. Thank you.

To the rest of the Farmer J Food team, Alice and Tomer, this book is stronger because of you.

Alice, my best friend and my safe place. You've kept me sane through this and through life in general. Thank you for the laughs, for your leeks, and for showing up every single time.

Tomer, you've got an eye for flavour and a brain for balance. Thank you for your detail, your freekancini and for just getting it.

Also a massive thanks to the Farmer J chefs that came before: Nick Sandler and Shuli Wimer. Nick, your whole roasted cauliflower and kale miso slaw are legendary. Shuli, you bring joy into every kitchen you walk into. Your tuna tartare lives on in this book and in our hearts.

To Oli, Lucie and Meytar – my team, my people. You've been everything. Calm in the chaos, energy when mine was gone, and endlessly good at what you do. Couldn't have done this without you.

To the whole Farmer J crew, in the kitchens, behind the tills and counters, in the head office – you are the ones who make the magic happen, day in and day out. And to our customers – thank you for choosing to eat with us, for loving food the way we do, and for inspiring us to keep going. This one's for you too.

To Thom Atkinson, our incredible, long-standing Farmer J photographer. You nailed it Again.

To our PR team, especially Emily Austen. Thank you for the permanent encouragement. You're an inspiration and I'm endlessly grateful for you.

To Elizabeth and Izzy at Penguin, thank you for believing in this book and backing it so brilliantly. You've been a joy to work with and here's to the next one.

To Jess Price, whose illustrations dance off the page – thank you for bringing the Farmer J spirit to life. To Sophie Yamamoto, who designed this book - thank you for understanding our vision and making my pattern dream come true.

To Jesse, who somehow holds it all together: without you, I'd be completely lost; thank you for being you: I wouldn't have been able to write this book without your support.

To my friends and family. Thank you for being our at-home recipe testers. To my mother-in-law, the original source of many a Farmer J flavour. You're the reason Jonathan fell in love with food. To my parents, thank you for making me who I am. Mummy, for being the strong and beautiful force you are, always with a cause, and always fighting in my corner, thank you for your belief in me, Jonathan and Farmer J.

Dad, I wish you were well enough to read this. Though, knowing you, you wouldn't have cooked any of it. Seasonal produce was your thing, but bold flavours? Not so much. (Some consolation, I guess.) And finally, to Rafa, Noa and Boaz, this book was written for grown-ups, but one day I hope you'll eat from it. And maybe even enjoy it. No more plain pasta, please. I'm forking begging you.

# From Jonathan

First of all I want to thank my wife, my partner in life and work, Ali. Without you nothing would be possible. You are a source of inspiration, your energy is larger than life and without you, I would find life much (much) harder. Seeing you write this book left me in awe . . . while running your normal day job and being the mother of our three little kids. You are just incredible and I am grateful for every second that we are married and working together.

Ever since I was born, food has been the main event – the focal point of nearly every memory in my life. And that's largely thanks to my parents, especially my mom. She's always been the most creative person I know, and the kitchen is where much of that creativity comes to life. Her cooking is nothing short of art – every meal felt like a celebration, with a table full of dishes bursting with flavour. From slow-roasted meats to vibrant, colourful salads . . . from rich pastas and indulgent risottos to perfectly balanced seafood dishes – there was always variety, always depth, and always her unique twist. And above all, she used the best ingredients she could find. Mom, I wanted to thank you for cooking something different for us every night of the week..

To my dad, you've always been my support and my confidant, and I'm so grateful for your encouragement when I decided to leave my stable job at the bank and start the Farmer J adventure. Thanks for being part of this journey. A passion for food and amazing restaurants is definitely something I got from you.

To my brother, I still remember our chat in 2013 at that fancy hotel in London while I was still working at the bank. You asked me why I didn't start a food business, and you convinced me that it could be a huge success. You've always been such a great sounding board, and I really appreciate your advice.

My sister, thank you for eating my food while we were growing up! The sesame soy chicken (Sticky Chicken Thighs on page 106) in the book is inspired by you.

Grandma, thank you for the famous leek and potato soup, homemade sun-dried tomatoes, and the most amazing home-grown tomatoes and basil – your vegetable garden back in Brookville is one of my aspirations in life!

# From Nitai

To my parents, Orly and Eitan – the first to believe my love for food was more than a hobby. To my father, who took us to restaurants when other kids were fast asleep. Who taught me friendship, hospitality, and the beauty of cooking slow, with patience, with spice, and with joy. To my mother, the teacher with a green thumb and a kind heart. You showed me sustainability before it was cool, the value of helping others, and that being humble is a quiet kind of power.

To Giada, my wife, my partner in crime, my beautiful force of nature. Without you, I wouldn't be the man I am. You are the Parmesan to my pasta, the tahini in my hummus.

To Aner and Saray, my older brother, my younger sister – my yin and yang in this journey. And to our whole family back home.

To my grandparents, Ester and Shlomo, Avraham and Sarah, thank you for the memories I'll carry for ever. You are the original story I try to tell through food. 'Thank you' will never be enough.

To the generations of chefs who pass on their knowledge, passion and spirit. To friends in this wild, almost impossible profession. To the farmers, growers, suppliers and all those backstage, fuelling the machine we call the food world.

To my dear friends in London and across the globe and especially the ones from home.

And finally, to my daughter, Eleonora – a sunbeam lighting our lives, giving everything deeper meaning. Dada loves you, much much.

EBURY PRESS

UK | USA | Canada | Ireland | Australia
India | New Zealand | South Africa

Ebury Press is part of the Penguin Random House group
of companies whose addresses can be found at
global.penguinrandomhouse.com

Penguin Random House UK
One Embassy Gardens, 8 Viaduct Gardens, London SW11 7BW

penguin.co.uk
global.penguinrandomhouse.com

First published by Ebury Press in 2026
1
Copyright © Ali Recanati, Jonathan Recanati, Nitai Shevach 2026
Illustrations © Jess Price, Farmer J 2026
Photography © Thom Atkinson 2026

The moral right of the author has been asserted.

Penguin Random House values and supports copyright. Copyright fuels creativity, encourages diverse voices, promotes freedom of expression and supports a vibrant culture. Thank you for purchasing an authorised edition of this book and for respecting intellectual property laws by not reproducing, scanning or distributing any part of it by any means without permission. You are supporting authors and enabling Penguin Random House to continue to publish books for everyone. No part of this book may be used or reproduced in any manner for the purpose of training artificial intelligence technologies or systems. In accordance with Article 4(3) of the DSM Directive 2019/790, Penguin Random House expressly reserves this work from the text and data mining exception.

Publishing Director: Elizabeth Bond
Editor: Izzy Frost
Production Controller: Percie Bridgwater
Designer: maru studio G.K.
Photographer: Thom Atkinson
Food Stylists: Nitai Shevach and Anna Williams
Prop Stylist: Hannah Wilkinson
Copyeditor: Clare Sayer
Proofreader: Maggie Ramsay
Indexer: Lisa Footitt

Colour origination by Altaimage Ltd
Printed and bound in China by C&C Offset Printing Co., Ltd

The authorised representative in the EEA is Penguin Random House Ireland, Morrison Chambers, 32 Nassau Street, Dublin D02 YH68.

A CIP catalogue record for this book is available from the British Library

ISBN 9781529955132

 Penguin Random House is committed to a sustainable future for our business, our readers and our planet. This book is made from Forest Stewardship Council® certified paper.